Otto Rentz, Dominik Möst, Anke Eßer (Eds.)

Current Development of Green IPPs: Experiences, Challenges and Strategies

Workshop of the EC-ASEAN Green

Independent Power Producers Network

15th of September, 2005 in Karlsruhe

Current Development of Green IPPs: Experiences, Challenges, and Strategies

Workshop of the EC-ASEAN Green Independent Power Producers Network
15th of September, 2005 in Karlsruhe

Otto Rentz
Dominik Möst
Anke Eßer
(Eds.)

universitätsverlag karlsruhe

Impressum

Universitätsverlag Karlsruhe
c/o Universitätsbibliothek
Straße am Forum 2
D-76131 Karlsruhe
www.uvka.de

Universitätsverlag Karlsruhe 2005
Print on Demand

ISBN 3-937300-73-2

Preface

Due to growing environmental issues, a strong political will to increase the use of renewable energy sources in energy supply exists in many countries of the world. Mainly in the European Union, measures to promote renewable energy projects have been taken. Inter alia special policy actions aiming at fostering renewable energy projects have been implemented. In Asia, the use of renewable energy is being promoted, too. However, policies as well as markets are still rather in the fledging stages when compared to Europe.

Therefore, the Asia-Europe Meeting – Green Independent Power Producers Network (ASEM Gripp Net) was set up as a thematic network on Green IPPs, to transfer experiences made in European power markets with success factors and market potentials of renewable energy projects to Southeast Asia. In doing so it links researchers, industry representatives, policy makers, and NGOs from Europe and Southeast Asia. The renewable energy projects considered within the network comprise wind, biomass combustion, biomass digestion, and small hydro power plant projects.

The network was funded within the Fifth Framework Program of the European Commission for a two year period. Within this period a website (http://www.ec-asean-greenippnetwork.net/) with regularly updated information about project outcomes was established, a quarterly newsletter was published and four workshops concerning different subjects in the green power business were held. The following six institutes set up the core of the ASEM Green IPP network:

- IIP (Institute for Industrial Production), Germany as coordinator,
- ECN (Energy research Centre of the Netherlands), Netherlands,
- Risoe (Risoe National Laboratory), Denmark,
- CEERD (Centre for Energy Environment Resources Development), Thailand,
- UPSL (University of the Philippines Solar Laboratory), Philippines, and
- ACE (ASEAN Centre for Energy), Indonesia.

They have teamed up in three thematic blocks, each block comprising one European and one Asian partner, who served as competence centres within the network.

Due to the successful implementation of the project, a funding for a continuation has been approved by the EAEF (EC-ASEAN Energy Facility). Within this continuation the institutionalization of the Green IPP Network in the ASEAN New and Renewable Sources of Energy Sub-Sector Network (NRSE SSN) is one of the main aims. Accordingly the network was named EC-ASEAN Green IIP Network. Besides, the publication of the quarterly newsletter continues and further workshops dealing with topics in the renewable energy business are organized. Furthermore, two partners joined the network:

- PTM (Pusat Tenaga Malaysia or Malaysia Energy Center), who is coordinator of the ASEAN Renewable Energy Sub-sector Network (RE-SSN) and also of the EC-ASEAN Green IPP network, and
- IMA (Informatics Management Associates), Thailand.

The book at hand contains a combination of several works and research activities in the field of renewable energies, which have been presented on the EC-ASEAN Green IPP Network workshop *"Current Development of Green IPPs* (Independent Power Producers)*: Experiences, Challenges, and Strategies"* in Karlsruhe. The workshop in September 2005 was organized by the Institute for Industrial Production (IIP), Universität Karlsruhe (TH). The contributions can be classified in three topics:

- renewable energy technologies and resources (Dhainaut et al., Koch et al., Champel)
- economic and policy context for renewable energy development (Möst et al., Held et al., Negro et al.)
- emission trading and CDM (Eßer et al., Dang et al., Bakker)

We are grateful to the EC-ASEAN Energy facility for making this workshop possible and we would like to thank all individuals and institutions, who have contributed to the success of the workshop.

Karlsruhe, September 2005

The editors

Table of Contents

Biogas recovering with microturbines and gas engines: Specificities and experience feedback

Thierry Dhainaut, Sébastien Cassen, Sylvain Martino and Eric Plantive
European Institute for Energy Research, Karlsruhe, Germany

ABSTRACT: Biogas recovering is becoming a major concern worldwide, due to environmental policies promoting renewable energy sources (RES) integration within the urban fabric, greenhouse effect gases (GEG) reduction or sustainable waste treatment processes, such as anaerobic digestion (AD). Meanwhile, Distributed Energy Resources techniques, as an alternative to conventional energy planning, offer appealing prospects such as conversion of renewables for electricity generation. Biogas recovering solutions are almost mature but on-site integration of prime-movers (gas engines, microturbines, etc.) together with their peripherals needs to be thoroughly worked out in order to improve plant reliability and economics. During this R&D project, available biogas fired technologies has been assessed through a step-by-step process (laboratory testing, field trials, and accompaniment of commercial projects) aiming at successively analyzing the energy and environmental performance of these systems, their flexibility facing such varying gases, integration constraints in technical, economic and administrative terms, and finally the functional ability of complete units. Economic and technical data of operational pilot plants have been gathered for various biogases (sewage gas, landfill gas and agricultural digester gas) and two different technologies (30 kWe microturbine and 22 kWe gas engine).

1 Introduction

Jointly created in September 2001 by Electricité de France (EDF) and the University of Karlsruhe, the European Institute for Energy Research (EIfER) has chosen to orientate its efforts towards the topics of Distributed Resources and Sustainable Development of cities and territories. Biogas recovering, which presents real stakes in term of RES mobilization as well as GEG emission decreasing, lies within the heart of EIfER concerns. Its activities in this field aim to identify and experiment cost-effective and reliable biogas recovering solutions, including microturbines and gas engines. In order to figure out integration and O&M constraints for these emerging technologies, EIfER works closely with EDF Group entities, such as VERDESIS, or makes partnerships with public or commercial players, such as local communities or farmers, on exemplary operations.

2 Microturbine technology presentation

Specificities. Microturbines are small internal combustion turbines, with an electrical power output within the [30 ;250] kW range. As most of internal combustion turbines, these turbo-generators are able to run on various fuels and are well-sized for commercial CHP applications or single electricity supplying to tertiary or industrial customers.

Whereas this kind of system consists mainly in a gas turbine, using the same fundamentals, it stands apart with unique features such as:

- A compact technology, so called "aeroderivative", initially used in the aeronautic sector (auxiliary power unit – APU – for aircraft on-board electricity generation), which limits the footprint;
- No mechanical reductor, as the turbine and the generator are mounted on the same high-speed shaft (up to 120.000 rpm);
- Oil-free operation for some models (Capstone), with air bearings, which is a real asset in term of maintenance;
- The use of a DC bus connected to a convertor (power electronics) to produce a 50Hz AC electrical current;
- The use of a recuperator on exhaust fumes in order to pre-heat air before the combustion chamber to keep a high internal temperature, which increases electrical efficiency up to 20 to 30%.

Functioning principle (cp. Figure 1)

1. Biogas, once sucked from the landfill cells or generated by a fermenter, is cleaned (sulphide removal with activated charcoal and dewatering) and then compressed (4 to 6bar).
2. Biogas is burnt into the microturbine combustion chamber, in mixture with pressurized air that has been sucked in and compressed at the microturbine inlet.
3. Exhaust gases are expanded through the turbine blades and their thermodynamic energy is converted into mechanical energy, and then into electrical energy by means of a high-speed alternator.
4. The high-frequency electricity is rectified and converted at 50Hz, using a power electronics interface, before being injected into the grid.
5. Heat losses, which are partially used for combustion air pre-heating (recuperator), may be recovered through an external heat exchanger for CHP (e.g. fermenter heating).

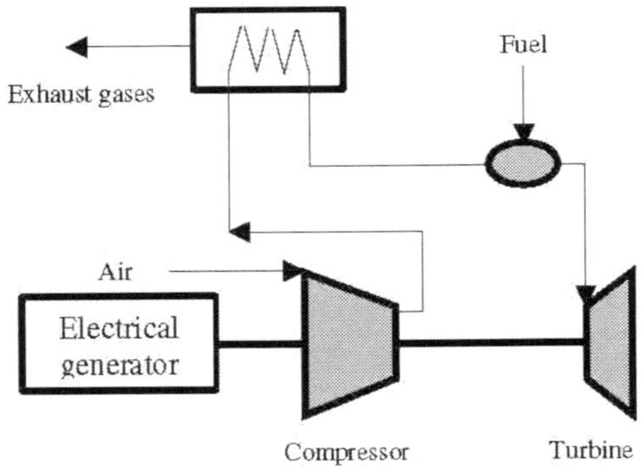

Figure 1: Functioning diagram of a microturbine

3 Preliminary laboratory testing

Testing procedure. The Capstone C30 microturbine is the main model that is commercially available in Europe for biogas recovering. This system is theoretically suitable for a large range of fuels thanks to an electronic interface that allows the adjustment of internal operating parameters according to the expected fuel composition. In order, on the one hand, to validate the performance announced by the manufacturer and, on the other hand, to anticipate the microturbine behaviour facing gas quality fluctuations, tests have been led by EDF R&D

Division by means of a methane – carbon dioxide mixing device to simulate any type of biogas, connected to a 6 bar storage tank to get rid of gas booster.

Figure 2: Microturbine test bench for performance assessment

The testing program has then made it possible to assess the microturbine suppleness during two measurement campaigns:

- Energy and environmental balance assessment, with continuous adjustment of the microturbine according to the "biogas" composition ;
- Sensitivity study, making the "biogas" composition vary around the same adjustment point.

Results. Tests have not only validated the performance that was announced by the US manufacturer but have also demonstrated the microturbine adaptability to a large range of biogas compositions, even significantly fluctuating.

Performance assessment with continuous adjustment of operating parameters

Performance is stable on the [35;70%] CH_4 content range, with a nearly constant electrical power of 29 to 30kW, for an efficiency of 25,3 to 26,9%.

Sensitivity study

Operation suppleness is very satisfying, with the possibility to run between -10 and +20pts of CH_4 content around the same adjustment point, with a steady efficiency of about 26% down to -7pts CH_4.

Emissions

Regarding environmental emissions, data are the following (with a 55% CH_4 adjustment) :

- NOx : 2 ppm @ 15% O_2
- CO_2 : 1,7% vol.
- CO : 22 ppm @ 15% O_2 (with $CO/CO_2 < 0,1$, indicating a clean combustion)
- Environmental performance is then quite good, but stays sensitive to load and/or methane content variations.

4 Microturbine field trials

Further to these preliminary laboratory tests, the Capstone microturbine has been installed on several pilot sites for field trials, in cooperation with Verdesis, in order to identify integration constraints for this kind of technology and to validate performance on real operating conditions.

4.1 Landfill gas: field trial on the landfill of Salmour (Italy)

Description. The microturbine has been firstly implemented on an end-of-life Italian landfill (at Salmour, Cuneo province), in parallel to a 250kW gas engine, running in limp-home mode at 160kW, due to insufficient biogas flow in addition to low methane content (between 47 and 53% CH_4). The unit, which has been set up out-door in 3 days in July 2002, consisted in a Copeland scroll gas booster, which was installed behind the existing cooling group (biogas dehydration by water condensing), together with the C30 microturbine equipped with a Capstone sour gas filter.

Experience feedback. This first experience has been globally positive with a 27kW electricity generation during more than 1.050 running hours, despite of extremely unfavourable weather conditions, notably with high external temperature leading to an efficiency dropping down to 24,5%, and lightening impacts onto the grid causing frequent electrical breaks. These unexpected breaks, by disconnecting the gas cooler, are probably at the origin of the early aging of the gas booster, which showed light oil leakages at the end of the field trial.

4.2 Sewage gas: field trial on the wastewater treatment plant of Frick (Switzerland)

Description. Further to Italian on-site testing campaign, the microturbine has been transferred to Switzerland, on the wastewater treatment plant of Frick, which is equipped of a sewage sludge mesophilic fermenter with a gasometer (Figure 3). The goal of this second field trial was to assess the opportunity of replacing the existing CHP modules that are powered by gas engines, the emissions of which being not any more compliant with the Swiss environmental regulation.

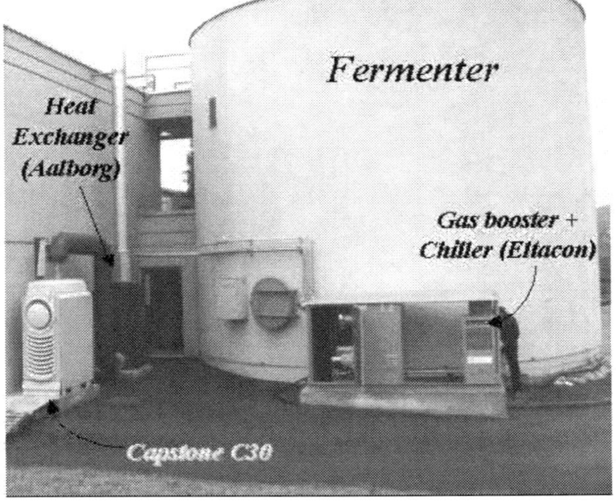

Figure 3: Frick (CH) wastewater treatment plant equipped with the biogas microturbine unit

A Danish Aalborg heat exchanger has then been added to the microturbine to recover exhaust fumes heat in order to ensure fermenter sludge heating. The Copeland gas booster has been replaced by a Dutch Eltacon integrated skid, gathering a cooler with a gas booster (Figure 4). An automatic switch-off device has been implemented to stop the unit in case of low biogas level inside the fermenter: for safety reasons, the unit was started again manually, requiring a service technician on-site.

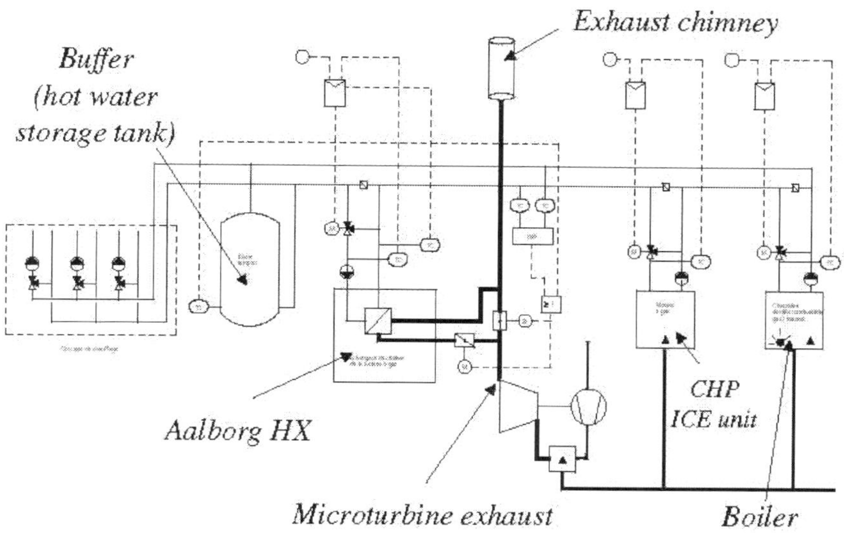

Figure 4: Hydraulic piping diagram

Experience feedback. The unit has been operated during 500 hours with satisfying performance. Figure 5 shows the influence of weather conditions on the microturbine efficiency, which slightly diminishes as outside temperature increases.

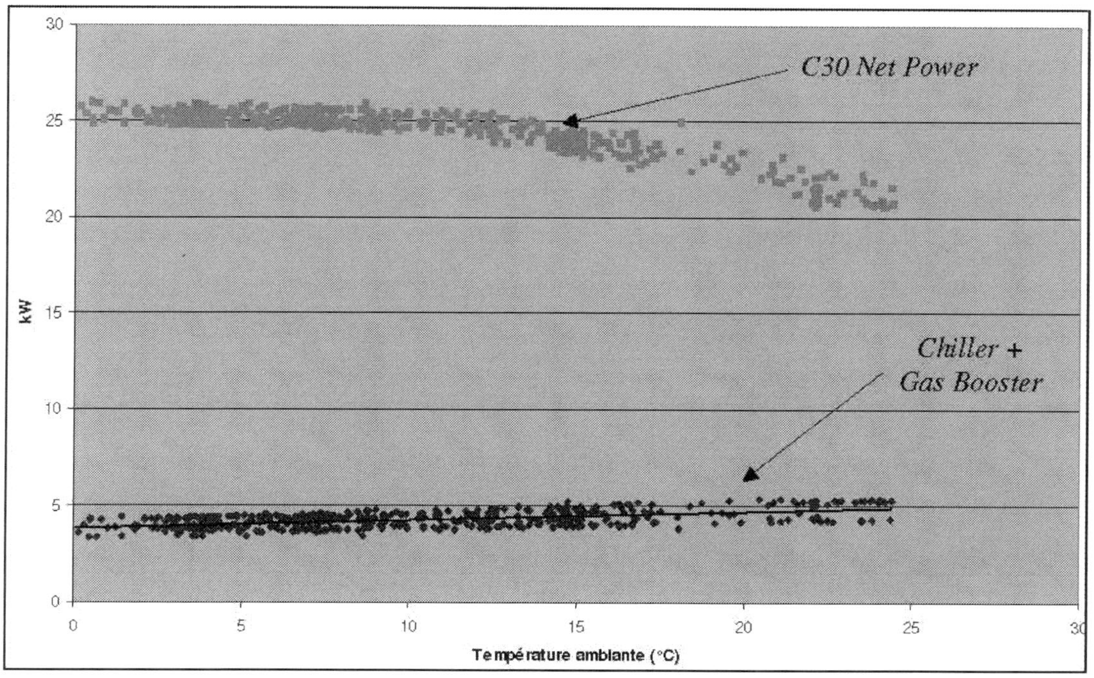

Figure 5: C30 microturbine net electrical output vs. ambient temperature

The experience feedback has pointed up the importance of a strict unit designing, particularly regarding peripherals. Thus, the heat exchanger internal by-pass showed a lack in term of modulation ability, as the minimum flow was not low enough to prevent from sludge over-heating. An external by-pass has then been added directly from the microturbine outlet to the heat exchanger chimney, in order to evacuate the whole heat without heating sludge. Besides, optimisation pathways of the Eltacon module have also been highlighted, concerning control panel venting failure and insufficient condensate draining at the cooler outlet. Lastly, performance monitoring has been handicapped by faulty GSM transmissions.

Costs. The investment cost-breakdown is detailed hereafter:

- Equipment:	€ 85.700
• µGT C30 (2001) + Fuel kit : € 53.200	
• Eltacon unit : € 18.000	
• Aalborg HX : € 9.800	
• Alterations : € 4.700	
- Installation:	€ 38.990
• Authorizations : € 2.500	
• Civil works : € 3.600	
• Connections : €32.890	
- R&D costs:	€ 22.800
• Instrumentation : € 20.800	
• Gas analysis : € 2.000	
TOTAL:	***€ 147.490***

As some items, such as equipment alterations and R&D costs, are fully related to the pilot plant and shall be deleted for future commercial units, the specific investment cost with the updated Capstone microturbine price is about 3.300€/kWe.

5 Accompaniment of commercial projects

5.1 Landfill gas at Thieulloy L'Abbaye, France

Description. SMITOP is a local community, working as a public corporation, which holds waste treatment competency for 7 cantons of the administrative department of Somme, 4 cantons of Oise and one canton of Seine Maritime. Its territory represents 262 communes, mainly rural, with 96.800 inhabitants.

The SMITOP waste treatment plant (landfill, waste sorting and green waste composting platform) includes a former landfill cell that has been used from 1982 to 2002. This section of 300.000 tons of household wastes forms the cell on which the biogas recovering will be firstly operated. The SMITOP landfill gas recovering installation consists of 8 industrial packaged C30 microturbines, connected to a Pioneer unit, for biogas cleaning and compressing, and to a Cain heat exchanger for heat losses recovering (CHP architecture, see Figure 6).

Technological choice. Microturbines have been chosen according to several criteria:

- Environmentally speaking, microturbines emit less pollutants than internal combustion engines;
- In term of modularity, the number of running microturbines may range from 1 to 8 according to landfill gas production;

- Operating suppleness is better, as microturbines can recover fluctuating composition biogas easier than gas engines, even for low methane content (down to 35% CH_4).

Figure 6: SMITOP's 8-microturbine plant

EDF, notably through EIfER institute, is a technical partner of this European "premiere" inaugurated on September 30th, 2004, and which has benefited from subsidies from the French government, for a total investment cost of 850.000€. The payback period is about 5 to 6 years, including grants, especially thanks to green electricity resale to the EDF grid.

First experience feedback. The biogas plant is operational since June 2004 but its functioning is limited by a big amount of water (leachates) inside the landfill cell, which prevent from an optimal biogas generation and does not permit a normal gas supply to the microturbines, the performance of which being separately satisfying. Moreover, a mutual management system has been implemented. Alternative outputs for heat are also studied with a view to optimise heat losses recovering, in addition to facilities heating.

5.2 Agricultural biogas at Mignéville, France

Description. EIfER accompanies another commercial biogas project on a farm-scale anaerobic digestion plant in Lorraine (France), at the "Les Brimbelles" smallholding at Mignéville. The AD plant generates biogas from agricultural wastes (slurry and manure coming from 65 dairy cows), which is recovered through a gas engine powered CHP module of 22kWe. The biogas plant has been built according to a German pattern (Kompogas process). It consists of two airtight concrete tanks: the first one (235m^3) is the fermenter itself that is intermittently mixed and heated in mesophilic mode (35-37°C), and the second one (338m^3) is more a storage tank, collecting the surplus coming from the fermenter when adding fresh substrate and covered with synthetic rubber membrane to store the biogas. A picture of this plant is shown at Figure 7.

The biogas recovering CHP module is manufactured by the Czech company TEDOM, and is composed of a Skoda gas converted car engine directly coupled to an asynchronous generator, fully integrated in a soundproof package (Figure 8). Heat is recuperated on the exhaust fumes and on the cooling water of the gas engine, through a 70/90°C hot water secondary circuit. This hot water is used to heat the fermenter up to 37°C approx., as well as the cowshed and the farmer house, which was previously wood-heated. Equipped with two gas lines and a modem communication device, cost was about €19.900 in 2002.

Figure 7: « Les Brimbelles » farm-scale AD plant

Figure 8: TEDOM CHP module

Experience feedback. The unit has been firstly commissioned in September 30th, 2003, with propane, in order to provide enough heat to the digester to get a steady biogas production. The fuel line has been switched to biogas in mid-December 2003. Because of fermenter airtightness issues, the unit has run in limp-home mode until summer 2004, with low methane content into the biogas (about 34% at the gas engine inlet) due to air succion through the fermenter concrete. This problem has been fixed by using a special polyurethane based mastic and by adding a pressure probe into the fermenter to automatically stop the engine in case of total biogas emptying. A small air pump has also been added onto the gas line to get rid of hydrogen sulphide, which has already corroded the plate heat exchanger once. Methane content is now 58% approx., oxygen free.

Performance. Since September 2003, the biogas CHP electricity, which has been resold to the EDF grid at 7,7c€/kWhe (see Figure 9). Its functioning is now fully satisfying, in term of performance as well as reliability, even if this technology requires frequent maintenance (notably oil changes every 400 operating hours extended to 650h). Average electrical output is 20kW, with a gross efficiency of 24,5%, which is below the manufacturer announcement of 28%, and a net efficiency of 23,9%. Global efficiency, including thermal energy recovering, is 80% (no additional cooler is used).

Some improvements of the AD plant are regarded in order to reach a 24h-a-day biogas production and then to maximize gas engine running hours, by adding co-substrates such as vegetal fat or lactoserum (co-digestion).

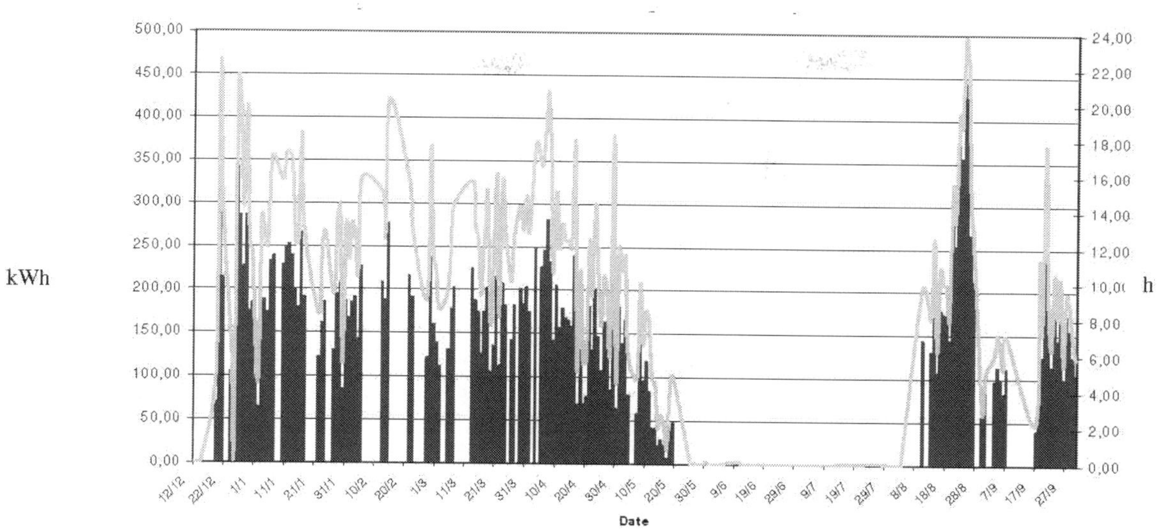

Figure 9: Average daily electrical energy supplied by the gas engine running on biogas (dark grey) and operating hours (light grey) over one year

6 Conclusion

Microturbines: still an "emerging" technology?

Optimum biogas recovering require to properly master fluctuations in term of flow and/or composition of these gases that may potentially contain harmful corrosive compounds. Microturbines give the possibility to handle these constraints and even to recover very low calorific value biogases, provided that designing and integration of the various peripherals are watchfully done. Nevertheless, this innovative technology remains costly and the upcoming of midsize systems soon on the market should improve their commercial development.

Microturbines: a complementary offer besides gas engines

Gas engine technology, though it requires frequent maintenance due to oil lubrication and needs to be cooled down even if there is no heat usage, has demonstrated its robustness and cost-effectiveness, provided that biogas methane content is high enough.

7 Acknowledgements

Authors would like to thank all their partners for their involvement in making these pilot units successful, and in particular: Xavier Lombard and Beat Näf from Verdesis, Adiouma Sow from SMITOP, Francis Claudepierre from EARL *Les Brimbelles*, Jean-Jacques Faujanet from Eurotrading, and the whole staff of OPP and SPE Departments at EDF R&D.

8 References

Lombard X., Courcelle B., Dhainaut T., Lora-Ronco T., Palmas G. and Bertolotto A. 2003. *Landfill Challenge*. Power Engineering International, 11(8):55-59.

Techno-economic Evaluation of Biomass Digestion Techniques and their optimised siting

Matthias Koch, Ute Karl, Michael Hiete and Otto Rentz
French-German Institute for Environmental Research (DFIU/IFARE),
Universität Karlsruhe (TH), Germany

ABSTRACT: The usage of biogas for electricity generation is still increasing in Germany due to the conditions guaranteed in the Renewable Energy Sources Act. Without transport, liquid raw materials show a higher energetic efficiency than solid materials due to the energy demand of preparing solid materials before digestion. With an increasing transport distance, the mass-specific energy content of the raw materials gets determining. Therefore, liquid materials should not be transported over longer distances. Plants operating with biodegradable wastes from municipalities (plant type W) are profitable mainly due to the received revenues for waste treatment. Plants operating with manure and regenerative raw materials (plant type A) profit only from the feed-in tariffs for electricity. High costs for cropping energy plants can lead to a deficit plant operation. The heavy metal concentrations of the residues of sewage sludge and manure can cause problems in the acceptance for the utilisation in agriculture.

1 Introduction

Biomass digestion is an anaerobic process that converts organic materials into biogas as well as solid and liquid residues. Most suitable for digestion is organic matter with a low lignin content, like e. g. liquid manure, non-wooden plants and sewage sludge. The biogas can be used for energy generation, mainly in small-scale combined heat and power plants (CHP). Depending on the content of pollutants, the residues may be used as organic fertiliser in agriculture or have to be disposed of in incineration plants.

Current situation in Germany: The theoretical annual biogas potential in Germany amounts to 15 billion m^3 of which 4.5 billion m^3 originates from liquid manure, 4.0 billion m^3 from agricultural residues (mainly straw, grass, beet leaf and haulm) and 3.7 billion m^3 from grown energy plants[1]. The biogas potential of organic wastes from industry, households and landscape conservation is 1.5 billion m^3 only. From sewage sludge 0.9 billion m^3 of sewage gas can be generated (cp. Table 1).

The German government introduced the "Renewable Energy Sources Act" in 2000 (with an update in 2004) to foster the renewable energy generation. This act guarantees feed-in tariffs for electricity generated from biogas and additional bonuses for electricity from combined heat and power generation (CHP), innovative technologies or if exclusively regenerative raw materials are used (Table 2). The feed-in tariffs are guaranteed for 20 years with a degression factor of 1.5% per year. For example, a biogas plant with liquid manure and regenerative raw materials as the only input materials and with an electrical CHP power below 150 kW will get 17.5 €ct/kWh in the first year.

[1] Based on the assumptions that energy plants are grown on 2 million ha and that one third of the energy plants (crops and grass) will be used for biogas generation (mixed cultivation).

Table 1: Theoretical biogas potential in Germany (Hartmann & Kaltschmitt, 2002)

Material	Amount [million Mg/a]	Biogas volume [billion m^3/a]	Energy content [PJ/a]
Liquid manure	162	4.5	97
Plant residues	23	4	86
Energy plants	9	3.7	80
Organic wastes	13	1.5	32
Sewage sludge	50	0.9	19
Total	257	15	314

Table 2: Feed-in tariffs for new biogas plant installations (first year) (EEG, 2004)

Size dependent feed-in tariffs	Fee paid [€ct/kWh]
- below 150 kW	11.5
- from 150 kW to 500 kW	9.9
- from 500 kW to 5 MW	8.9
- from 5 MW to 20 MW	8.4
Complementary payment for exclusive use of regenerative raw materials	
- up to 500 kW	6
- from 500 kW to 5 MW	4
Other complementary payments:	
- for CHP	2
- for innovative technologies	2

As a result of the guaranteed feed-in tariffs, the number of digestion plants increased from 850 installations in 1999 to 2500 in 2004. The total installed electrical capacity of the CHP of the biogas plants has increased in the same period from 45 MW to 430 MW. In 2004, 2.2 billion kWh electricity have been generated in Germany from biogas and sewage gas which amounted to a share of 0.3% of the total electricity demand. However, still only 10% of the theoretical biogas potential is actually used so that the number of plants and the electricity production are both expected to grow further (FNR, 2004; BEE, 2005; FVB, 2005).

Most of the installations are located in the agricultural sector. They are run by individual farmers or in cooperation with others using combinations of liquid manure and regenerative raw materials. The averaged installed electrical CHP power per new installation amounts to 150 kW (FNR, 2004).

About 50 installations are operating with biological waste. With an average throughput of 70,000 Mg/a, these plants treat together 20% of the biological waste in Germany (3.5 million Mg/a). The remaining 80% are composted together with 4 million Mg/a of biodegradable waste from landscape conservation (ifeu, 2005).

Research. The variety of organic materials, their specific biogas potential and spatial availability on one hand, their transport as well as techno-economic issues of the digestion plant on the other hand call for an optimisation of the whole supply chain including an optimised siting of the plant.

The research described here is supported by a grant of Volkswagen Foundation[2] and is performed in cooperation with GeoForschungsZentrum Potsdam (Dr. Hilke Würdemann).

2 Materials and Methods

To assess the suitability of different organic materials for biogas production, a process chain model with the relevant mass and energy flows was developed. The process chain was described as a Petri network[3] using the software tool Umberto®. Two plant types, one for agricultural raw materials (plant type A) and one for biological wastes (plant type W) were considered.

The network of plant type W comprises input material transport with heavy goods vehicles (HGV), represented as so-called transitions. At the plant site, further transitions for material preparation (sorting, pulper, hygienisation), digestion (reactor) and downstream treatment (dewatering) follow. The output material transport transition (with HGV) represents the end of the process chain. Biodegradable waste from municipalities, leftover, sewage sludge and liquid manure of cattle and pigs are used as input materials.

Plant type A accepts only liquid manure as well as corn and grass silage, in order to ensure the bonus for regenerative raw materials. The network consists of input material transport transitions with agricultural tractors, a collecting pit transition for liquid manure, the reactor, an entry transition for solid materials by a wheel-mounted front-end loader and an output material transport transition with agricultural tractors for liquid residues. Corn and grass cropping is represented by an upstream process chain.

The reactor type is identical for both plant types (temp. 38°C, dry matter concentration < 15%). Plant type W has a more intensive part of material preparation than plant type A but no upstream process chain for regenerative material cropping included as in plant type A.

The complete mass and energy flows are calculated for the various input materials. Their indicators are calculated from the input-output balances of each process chain configuration, quantifying the efficiency in economic and energetic terms. The heavy metal concentrations of the output flows indicate their suitability for agricultural utilisation.

The overall energetic efficiency is represented by the cumulated energy demand (CED). In this work, the CED includes only the energy demand for operating the plant. The CED consists of the electricity and diesel consumption and the CED of fertiliser and pesticide production. It is calculated by a simulation of the plant operation with material mono-charges. For co-digestion configurations, the CED can be combined linear.

The economic efficiency is calculated by cost comparison for a given period in time. This period is the average of 20 years of plant operation including changes of costs and revenues. Total investments for the plants are calculated based on the installed electrical CHP power and the reactor volume. Economy of scale is allowed for. Operating costs include material and personnel costs as well as costs for maintenance, capital and insurance.

The correlation of economic efficiency and the combination of various input materials is not linear (scale up), so the economic indicators are calculated exemplarily for special co-

---

[2] "Optimierung der Co-Vergärung in Bezug auf die spezifische Biogasbildung, die Produktqualität und ihre Einbindung in regionale Entsorgungskonzepte".

[3] A Petri network is a bipartite and directed graph containing places, transitions and arrows.

digestion configurations. Plant type A is therefore run by a mixture of two third liquid manure and one third of energy plant silage while plant type W is run either on sewage sludge or liquid manure basis with biodegradable municipal waste as additional material. The heavy metal concentration of the output flows is calculated for these configurations as well.

3 Results

3.1 Energetic efficiency.

The CED in terms of electricity, diesel and grass and corn cultivation for the plant operation are shown in Table 3. The thermal energy demand is not considered due to a surplus of thermal energy for all materials and a non-guaranteed purchase.

Table 3: Calculated cumulated energy demand (CED) of plant type W and A operation (without transport)

	CED plant type W (biowaste) [kWh/m³]	**CED plant type A (agriculture) [kWh/m³]**		
	Electricity	Electricity	Diesel	Fertiliser and pesticide production
Municipal biowaste	1.09	-	-	-
Municipal green waste	0.8	-	-	-
Sewage sludge	0.36	-	-	-
Leftover	0.68	-	-	-
Cattle liquid manure	0.24	0.17	0	0
Pig liquid manure	0.27	0.19	0	0
Grass silage	-	0.03	0.35	0
Corn silage	-	0.02	0.25	0.87

The CED increases with the transport distance. The slope is material specific and illustrated in Fugure 1 and Figure 2 for plant type W and A respectively. For an electrical efficiency of 35% of the CHP, a CED of 3.5 kWh/m^3 equals the electricity generated from one cubic metre methane ("electricity equivalent").

For plant type W, the slopes of the CED functions for liquid materials are about three times higher than the slopes for the solid ones. The y-axis intercepts of the solid materials consist mainly of the energy demand for material preparation.

For plant type A, the slopes of the CED functions for manure are about ten times higher than the slope for corn silage and five times higher than for grass silage. The high y-axis intercept of corn silage results mainly from the CED of fertiliser and pesticide production.

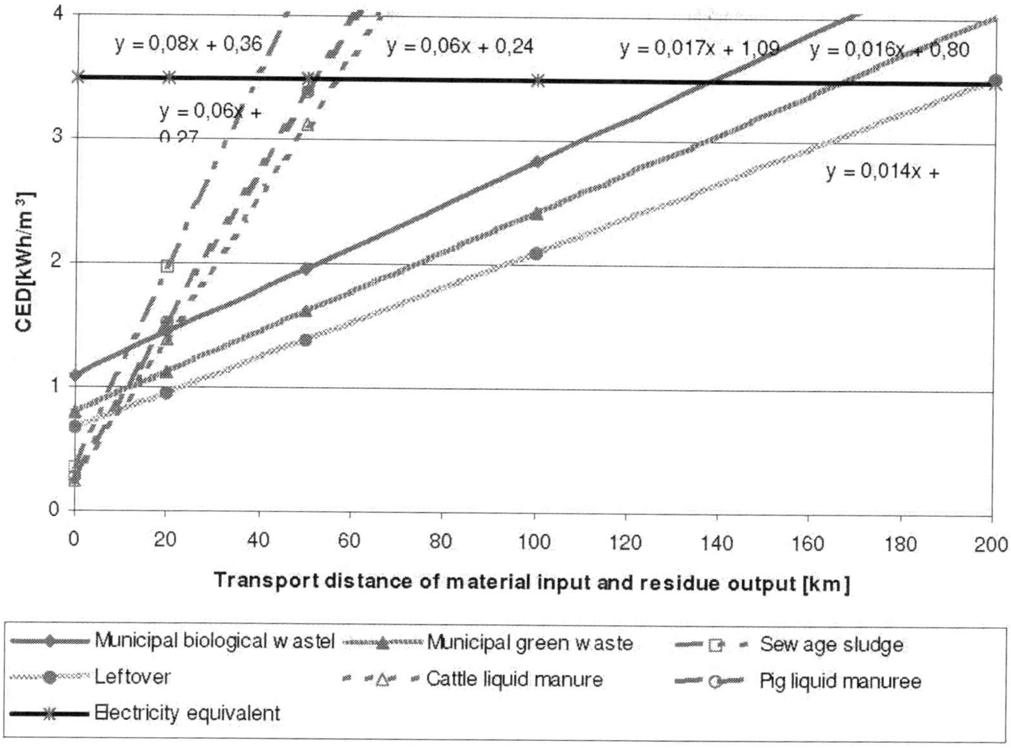

Figure 1: Material specific calculated CED of operating plant type W as a function of transport distance.

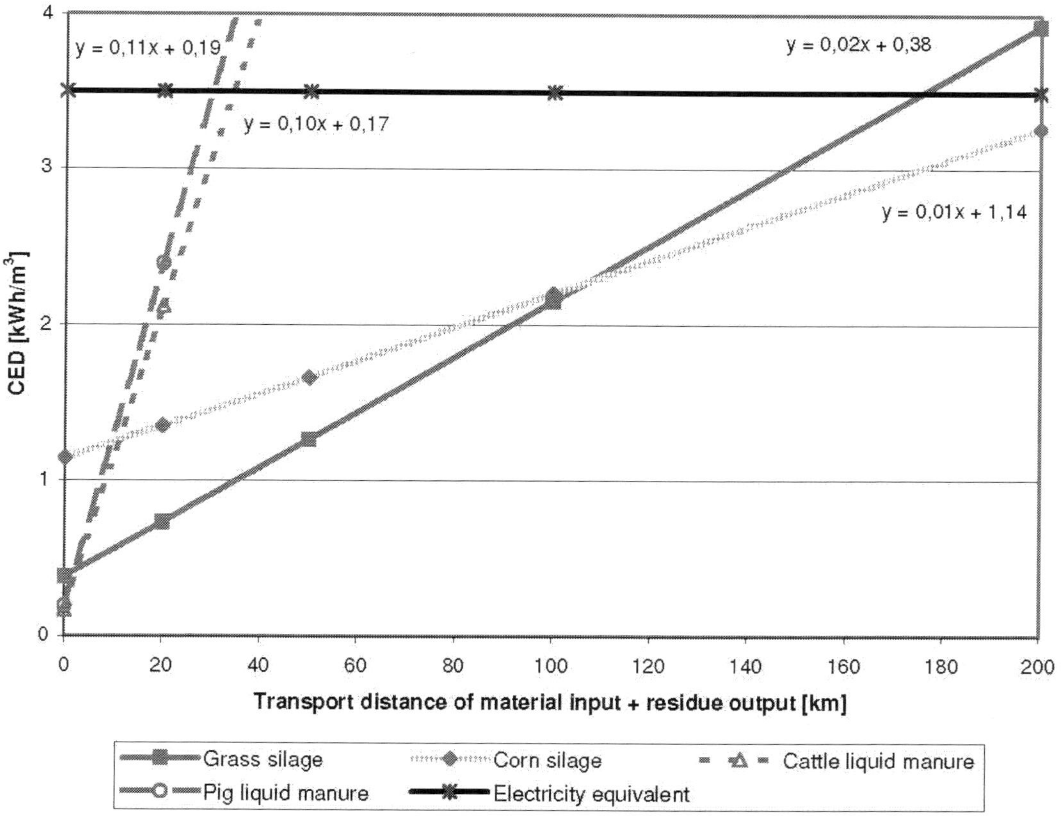

Figure 2: Material specific calculated CED of operating plant type A as a function of transport distance.

3.2 Economic efficiency.

Economy of scale is considered via EQUATION 1 with an exponent *m* of 0.67. As a base, specific investments of 2500 €/kW for a 150 kW plant power of plant type A and 4000 €/kW for a 1500 kW plant power of plant type W were assumed (FNR, 2004).

$$I_1 = I_2 \cdot \left[\frac{c1}{c2}\right]^m$$

I_1 = investment plant 1

I_2 = investment plant 2 **(EQUATION 1)**

c_1 = power plant 1

c_2 = power plant 2

m = scale-up exponent of 0.67

The assumed costs of plant operation are linked with an inflation rate of 1% and listed in Table 4 for the first year.

Table 4: Costs of plant operation in the first year (ASUE, 2005; FNR, 2004)

Maintenance	
- Plant buildings	0.5% of investment
- Installation engineering	$4.9406 \cdot P_{el}^{0.2219}$ €Ct/kWh$_{el}$
- General overhaul CHP (in the fifth engine year)	$79.77 \cdot P_{el} + 16534$ €
Supplies	
- Water	1.7 €/m^3
- Conditioning material	5 €/kg
- Diesel	0.8 €/L
- Electricity	10 €/MWh
Regenerative raw materials	
- Corn silage	25 €/Mg
- Grass silage	35 €/Mg
Charges	
- Waste water	2.2 €/m^3
- Waste	100 €/Mg
Wages and salaries	
- plant type A (farmer)	15 €/h
- plant type W (worker)	36000 €/a
Insurance	0.5% of total investment

The calculated profit and loss situation for plant type A and W are shown in Table 5 and Table 6 respectively.

For the configuration of liquid manure and corn silage, the profitable capacity starts from 7500 Mg/a (approx. 150 kW). The assumed production costs for grass silage are to high for a profitable plant operation in every capacity. To reach a loss-free plant operation for the same capacity (7500 Mg/a, approx. 120 kW), the costs for grass silage must not exceed 18 €/Mg.

Table 5: Profit and loss situation of plant type A, illustrated per Mg input and generated kWh electricity

Capacity	3000 Mg/a (approx. 55 kW)	9000 Mg/a (approx. 180 kW)	27000 Mg/a (approx. 630 kW)
Cattle liquid manure and corn silage (ratio 2:1)	-4.4 €/Mg -3.8 €Ct/kWh	1.1 €/Mg 0.8 €Ct/kWh	4.4 €/Mg 3.0 €Ct/kWh
Pig liquid manure and corn silage (ratio 2:1)	-4.6 €/Mg -4.1 €Ct/kWh	0.7 €/Mg 0.55 €Ct/kWh	4.0 €/Mg 2.8 €Ct/kWh
Capacity	**3000 Mg/a (approx. 45 kW)**	**9000 Mg/a (approx. 150 kW)**	**27000 Mg/a (approx. 500 kW)**
Cattle liquid manure and grass silage (ratio 2:1)	-10.2 €/Mg -11.3 €Ct/kWh	-5.7 €/Mg -5.6 €Ct/kWh	-2.8 €/Mg -2.4 €Ct/kWh
Pig liquid-manure and grass silage (ratio 2:1)	-10.4 €/Mg -12.0 €Ct/kWh	-6.0 €/Mg -6.1 €Ct/kWh	-3.1 €/Mg -2.8 €Ct/kWh

Table 6: Profit and loss situation of plant type W, illustrated per Mg input and generated kWh electricity (without revenues for material input and transport costs)

Capacity	15000 Mg/a (approx. 270 kW)	30000 Mg/a (approx. 550 kW)	60000 Mg/a (approx. 1200 kW)
Cattle liquid manure and municipal biowaste (2:1)	-25.0 €/Mg -20.5 €Ct/kWh	-20.4 €/Mg -16.8 €Ct/kWh	-16.8 €/Mg -13.8 €Ct/kWh
Pig liquid manure and municipal biowaste (2:1)	-24.7 €/Mg -22.8 €Ct/kWh	-20.5 €/Mg -17.4 €Ct/kWh	-16.9 €/Mg -14.3 €Ct/kWh
Capacity	**20000 Mg/a (approx. 270 kW)**	**40000 Mg/a (approx. 550 kW)**	**80000 Mg/a (approx. 1200 kW)**
Sewage sludge and municipal biowaste (3:1)	-19.3 €/Mg -22.8 €Ct/kWh	-16.0 €/Mg -17.5 €Ct/kWh	-13.3 €/Mg -14.5 €Ct/kWh

Every configuration of plant type W needs revenues for input materials for a profitable plant operation. If 60 €/Mg are assumed for biowaste, manure can be accepted for free to reach a loss-free plant operation in a capacity from 22500 Mg/a (approx. 400 kW). For sewage sludge 1 €/Mg has to be received to get the same result. Transport costs have to be included additionally as well. They may be assumed 0.20 – 0.50 € per Mg and kilometre for HGV transports (Koch, 2004).

The calculated heavy metal concentrations of the digestion residues from plant type A configurations allow in general the use in agriculture. Only pig liquid manure shows copper (+170%) and zinc (+85%) concentrations above the limit values of the German Ordinance on Biowastes (BioAbfV).

For plant type W, the input combination with pig liquid manure results in copper and zinc concentrations above the limit values of the German Ordinance on Biowastes (+260% for copper and +130% for zinc). The calculated heavy metal concentrations of sewage sludge and biowaste stay below the limit values of the Sewage Sludge Ordinance (AbfKlärV) in Germany. The use of digestion residues in agriculture will be discussed later on in more detail.

For waste water from plant type W configurations, only the calculated zinc concentrations exceed the limit values for waste water to discharge into public waste-water-treatment installations in Baden-Württemberg (+42% - +138%).

4 Discussion and conclusions

The water, energy and pollutant content of the input materials are main parameters that determine the suitability of these materials for digestion. Liquid raw materials like sewage sludge or manures have a low mass-specific energy content and therefore should not be transported over longer distances. For solid raw materials having a higher energy content transport is less critical (Figure 1 and Figure 2). For co-digestion plants a site near e.g. waste-water-treatment installations or livestock is favourable.

Another important item is material preparation. Liquid manure has a higher energy efficiency in plant type W configurations than biowaste within the first 10 km of transport distance due to unnecessary material preparation before digestion. Comparing liquid manure in plant type A and W without transport, it is more energy efficient to treat liquid manure in plant type A due to the unnecessary dewatering of the residues in plant type A. But above 20 km of transport distance, plant type W is getting more energy efficient for manure due to the reduced amount of residues after dewatering.

With an increasing plant size, all co-digestion plant configurations are getting more profitable. Plant type A is getting profitable for liquid manure and corn silage from a capacity of 7500 Mg/a (approx. 150 kW). For an equivalent profitable co-digestion of liquid manure and grass silage, the costs for grass silage have to be 18 €/Mg at most, which is nearly the half of the assumed costs. The operation of plant type A with grass silage and manure is not profitable in these conditions.

The calculated revenues for input materials at plant type W are within a realistic range. High revenues for manure can not be expected due to the general economic situation of the farmers in Germany: The economic situation of co-digestion plant type W depends mainly on the revenues for biowaste. A cooperation with farmers should include the utilisation of the digestion residues in agriculture. The operation of plant type W is profitable under the assumed terms and a capacity from 400 kW.

Although the digestion residues from the sewage sludge and biowaste combination do not exceed the limit values for heavy metals of the German Sewage Sludge Ordinance (AbfKlärV), their acceptance as a fertiliser is controversial. One reason is, that the limit values of the Sewage Sludge Ordinance are less strict than those of the Ordinance on Biowastes. If they get relevant, the residues from sewage sludge and biowaste will exceed the limit values for copper, mercury and zinc. The intensification of limit values for the utilisation of sewage sludge in agriculture is in discussion since years. These activities improve on the one hand the protection of soil and foods. On the other hand they might exclude the utilisation of digestion residues in agriculture and change therefore the conditions for biogas generation.

Outlook. The ecological efficiency concerning different environmental effects of the plant operation will be evaluated. Transport costs will be included in the economic evaluation. The optimisation of plant siting and plant sizing within the spatial context of the supply of organic materials and the capacity of using the digestion residues in agriculture will be further analysed using GAMS, a modelling tool for linear programming and optimisation. The transport distance matrices and the spatial allocation of input and output mass flows is calculated using a Geographic Information System (ArcGIS®).

5 References

Arbeitsgemeinschaft für umweltfreundlichen und rationellen Energieverbrauch e.V. (ASUE). 2005. *BHKW-Kenndaten 2005*. Kaiserslautern, pp.12-15.

Bundesverband Erneuerbare Energien e.V. (BEE). 17th June 2005. press release *Jahresprognose Biogas 2005: Strom für 3 Millionen Haushalte*. http://www.bee-ev.de/presse.php?pr=501

Erneuerbare-Energien-Gesetz (EEG) / Act on granting priority to renewable energy sources. 2004. Federal Law Gazette (Bundesgesetzblatt) 2004 I No. 40. 31st July 2004, Article 7.

Fachagentur für nachwachsende Rohstoffe (FNR) / Agency of Renewable Ressources. 2004. *Handreichung Biogasgewinnung und –nutzung*. Gülzow, pp.190-222.

Fachverband Biogas e.V. (FVB). 2005. 6th April 2005. press release *Daten und Fakten zur BioEnergie – Hintergrundpapier*. http://www.biogas.org/

Hartmann, H. and M. Kaltschmitt. 2002. *Biomasse als erneuerbarer Energieträger*. 2nd ed., Landwirtschaftsverlag GmbH, Münster, pp. 588-604

Institut für Energie- und Umweltforschung (ifeu) / Institute for Energy and Environmental Research. 2005. *Beitrag der Abfallwirtschaft zur nachhaltigen Entwicklung in Deutschland*. FKZ 203 92 309, p. 55.

Koch, M (2004). *Techno-ökonomische Analyse und GIS-gestützte Standortoptimierung von Co-Vergärungsanlagen*. Thesis, University of Karlsruhe, Germany, p. 72

Potential of Deep Aquifers for Geothermal Electricity Production in Alsace

B. Champel, L. Paredes
European Institute for Energy Research, Karlsruhe, Germany

ABSTRACT: The increasing interest for geothermics as a renewable energy source requires the development of geothermic resources analysis tools for heat and electricity production, as well as representation of the results in order to give reflection basis to the decision-makers. The aim of this study is to evaluate the resources stored in the French part of the deep aquifers in the Rhine Graben as well as to determine the location of favourable sites for the exploitation. We show that the resources are enormous in comparison to the electricity demand in the region. This study is now being extended to the other suitable French regions.

1 Introduction

As the international scientific community has proved that the present global warming is at least partly due to the increase of the atmospheric greenhouse gases, there is a growing need for higher energy efficient systems and for a development of renewable energies.

Several features make geothermics an interesting source of energy, among which:

- It is a clean and renewable energy source,
- it is independent of fuels (there is then no impact of price volatility),
- It is a baseload technology.

Geothermics is one of the renewable energy sources that addresses the two great energetic industries which are electricity and heat production. Until now, electricity production from geothermics was restricted to active geological zones where high geothermal gradients can be found. With the recent development of new conversion cycles (Organic Rankine Cycle or Kalina Cycle), medium enthalpy resources can be used for electricity production, as it is already the case in Austria (Altheim, Bad Blumau) since 2000-2001 or in Germany (Neustadt-Glewe) since 2003.

Due to the regional character of renewable resources distribution, regional planning authorities play a major role in the planning of future exploitation of renewable energies. The realisation of potential studies at a regional scale is thus fundamental for any further planning activities in the sector.

In France, the only geothermal plant producing electricity is situated in Bouillante in Guadeloupe and has been running since 1998. However, several aquifers constitute interesting resources for medium enthalpy geothermics. The aim of the study performed in EIfER was to develop a reproducible method for the evaluation of geothermics energy potential in Alsace, and the location of the most favourable sites for geothermics exploitation in this area.

2 Study area

The study area we chose lies in Alsace, in the French part of the Rhine Graben. The reasons for this choice are the already known geothermal potential of the region, but also the numerous available data concerning the subsurface. Indeed, the Rhine Graben is a moderately productive oil basin, that has been exploited during the past 150 years.

Geologically, the Rhine Graben corresponds to the central part of the European Cenozoic rift system which developed at the Oligocene time and extends from the Mediterranean Sea to the North Sea. This graben extends over a distance of 300 km from Basel to Frankfurt with an average width of 35 km. It is composed of several horsts and grabens. The Hercynian basement lies between 1200 m and 3500 m depth. It is overlapped by secondary sediments deposed from lower Triassic to Jurassic times. A subsequent emersion causes a total gap in the Cretaceous and a partial erosion of the Jurassic terrains. The tertiary subsidence of the basin led to a new sedimentary period. A new Miocene time emersion was followed by an alluvial filling.

In the Rhine Graben, three aquifers are likely to provide sufficiently hot water to produce electricity. They are from the bottom up (Figure 1):

- The Buntsandstein (lower Triassic), made of sandstone interfilled with clay.
- The Muschelkalk (mid Triassic), composed of clayey and sandy limestones and dolomites.
- The 'Grande Oolithe' (Bajocian and Bathonian), made of oolithic limestones, clayey at the base.

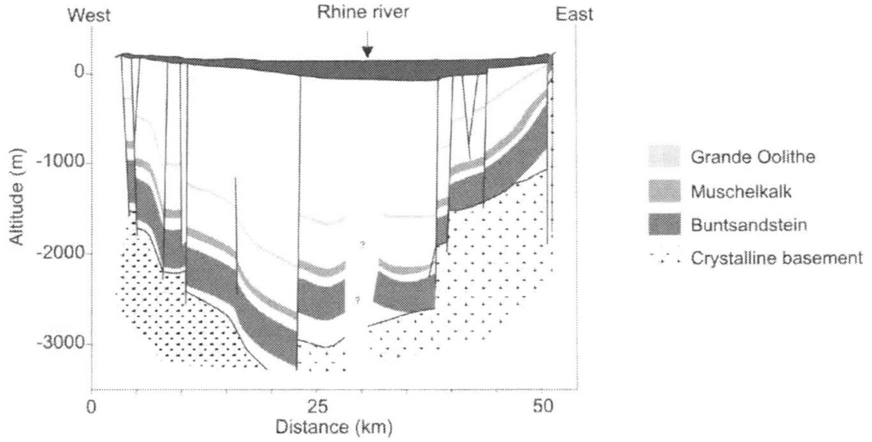

Figure 1: West-East cross-section of the Rhine Graben in the region of Strasbourg (modified after (Walgenwitz et al., 1979))

3 Determination of the available resources in the aquifers

3.1 Principle of the Calculation

The local potential of an aquifer for the electricity production can be calculated by the following formula (Jung et al., 2002; Kohl et al., 2003) with the explained parameters in Table 1:

$$E_{el} = \eta \, \rho_a \, C_a \, V \, (T_a - T_{in}) \tag{1}$$

3.2 Data Sets

This study used as a basis the maps included in "Synthèse Géothermique du Fossé Rhénan" (Walgenwitz et al., 1979). Local temperature and thickness of the three aquifers were determined after scanning and digitizing the corresponding maps. As a next step, an interpolation was realized with a spatial resolution of 500 m.

We supposed that only the zones where the aquifer temperature exceeds 100°C are suitable for electricity production. This limit is realistic but not absolute: for example, the installation of Neustadt-Glewe in Germany is fed by a brine of 98°C.

Table 1: Used parameters for calculating aquifers potential

Symbol	Explaination	Unit	Value
E_{el}	Potentially usable electrical energy	J	calculated
η	Heat / electricity conversion factor	∅	0,103
$\rho_a C_a$	Specific heat of the aquifer	$J / m^3 / K$	$2{,}38.10^6$
$\rho_w C_w$	Specific heat of the brine	$J / m^3 / K$	$4{,}18.10^6$
$\rho_r C_r$	Specific heat of the rock	$J / m^3 / K$	$2{,}18.10^6$
V	Volume of the aquifer	m^3	calculated
T_a	Aquifer temperature	°C	variable
T_{in}	Re-injected water temperature	°C	70
Δt	Doublet lifetime	Year	30
r_w	Borehole radius	m	0,1
s	Maximum admissible well drawdown	m	200
Tr	Aquifer transmissivity	m^2 / s	variable
h	Aquifer thickness	m	variable
k	Aquifer permeability	m / s	$1 - 5.10^{-7}$
Q	Production rate	m^3 / s	calculated
D	Inter-well distance	m	calculated

The values of the different parameters presented in equation (1) are determined locally for 500 m × 500 m cells. The heat in place and corresponding electricity potential are then calculated locally for each cell (Figure 2).

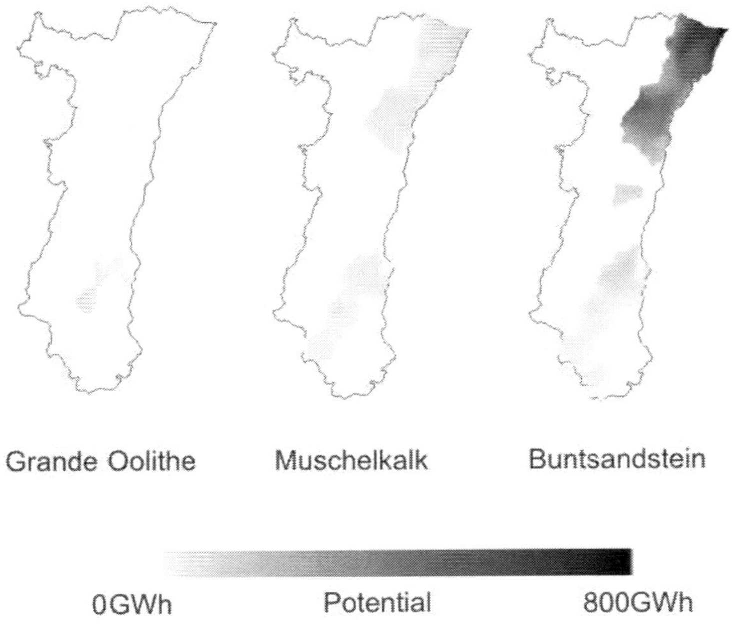

Figure 2: Electricity potential calculated for the three studied aquifers in Alsace

3.3 Calculation of the Theoretical Potential

The theoretical renewable energies potential includes all the physically available renewable energy sources which are suitable for energy use.

By integrating the electricity potential over the whole area, it is possible to calculate the total potential of each aquifer in the whole region (Table 2).

Table 2: Total electricity potential of the three aquifers in Alsace

Aquifer	Grande Oolithe	Muschelkalk	Buntsandstein
Potential (MWh)	$8{,}6.10^7$	$5{,}96.10^8$	$2{,}69.10^9$

By summing the potential of the three aquifers, the total potential for hydrothermal electricity production in Alsace can be calculated. This potential represents 3372 TWh, which is more than 250 times the annual electricity consumption in the region.

3.4 Calculation of Technical Potential

The technical renewable energy sources potential is the part of the theoretical potential that remains available for energy use when the existing technical and non technical limitations are taken into account.

In practice, the accessible resource that can be extracted is only a part of the total resource. The ratio depends on the availability of fluids in the aquifers (expressed by the transmissivity of the aquifer) and the time during which the extraction can be economically carried out.

An analytical expression derived by (Gringarten, 1978) links the thermal breakthrough time (supposed to be equal to the lifetime of the doublet Δt (s)) to the distance between the doublet wells D (m) and the production rate Q (m^3/s):

$$\frac{\rho_w C_w}{\rho_a C_a} \frac{Q \, \Delta t}{D^2 h} = \frac{\pi}{3} \tag{2}$$

with h the thickness of the aquifer (m) (see Table 1).

Another relationship between D, Q and the steady-state well drawdown s (m) is obtained from the theory of the potential derived from the Darcy law:

$$s = \frac{Q}{2\pi Tr} \ln \frac{D}{r_w} \tag{3}$$

with Tr the transmissivity of the aquifer (m²/s) and r_w (m) the intern radius of the borehole (see Table 1).

The key parameter in the former equation is the aquifer transmissivity (that is, its thickness times its permeability). For the aquifers of our study, only few data are available. Given the hazardous extrapolation of the existing values, we decided to use a spatially constant permeability for each of the aquifers. The transmissivity is then the product of this permeability and the thickness of the aquifer at a given point :

$$Tr = h k \tag{4}$$

Using the study of (Laurent, 1974), we chose a permeability (*k*) of 5.10^{-7} m/s for the Muschelkalk and 10^{-7} m/s for the Buntsandstein. We decided not to include the 'Grande Oolithe' in the further study, given its low potential, and its poor hydraulic properties.

The equations (2) and (3) can then be combined to calculate the optimal inter-well distance for each aquifer:

$$D^2 \ln\left(\frac{D}{r_w}\right) = 6 \frac{\rho_w C_w}{\rho_a C_a} \Delta t \, k \, s \tag{5}$$

With a lifetime of 30 years, a maximal admissible drawdown of 200 m and the above given permeabilities, the calculated optimal inter-well distance for the Muschelkalk is 349 m; for the Buntsandstein, it is 164 m.

The maximal flowrate is then given by:

$$Q = \frac{2\pi \, s \, h \, k}{\ln(D/r_w)} \tag{6}$$

The thermal power P_{th} of a geothermal plant is then given by:

$$P_{th} = Q \, \rho_w \, C_w \, (T_a - T_{in}) \tag{7}$$

and its electrical power P_{el} by:

$$P_{el} = \eta \, P_{th} \tag{8}$$

The local conceivable power that could be obtained with a geothermal doublet for the Muschelkalk and the Buntsandstein is shown in Figure 3.

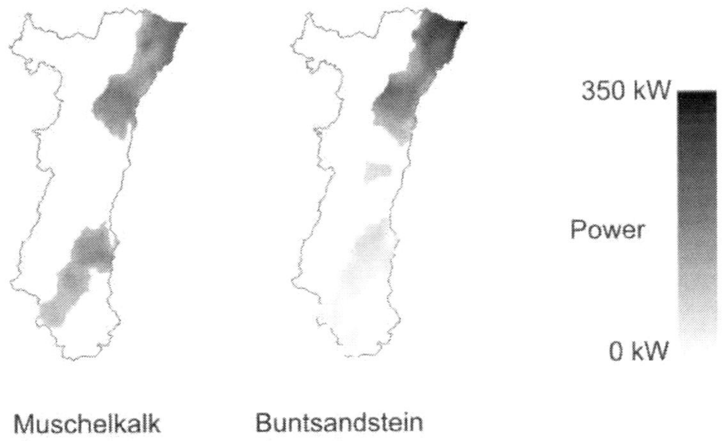

Figure 3: Electrical power of a plant fed by a single doublet in the Muschelkalk aquifer (left) and in the Buntsandstein aquifer (right)

The drainage area of this doublet is then related to the inter-well distance *D*. (Gringarten, 1978) has shown that the optimal configuration for the energy recovery from an aquifer was obtained with a five-spot pattern, for which the drainage area is $2D^2$. It is then possible to integrate the power of each single plant over the whole area of the study.

Summed over one year or over the whole lifetime of the plant, these results give the theoretical maximal energy that can be produced. The results of this integration are given in Table 3. The comparison of these results to the total energy stored in the aquifers permits to calculate a heat recovery factor of 51,6% for a 30-year exploitation (52,8% for a 100-year exploitation).

Table 3: Maximal theoretical energy that can be produced over the whole region during one year or during the whole lifetime of the plants

Lifetime	Annual production	Total production
30 years	58,0 TWh	1739 TWh
50 years	35,6 TWh	1780 TWh
100 years	17,8 TWh	1780 TWh

4 Location of most favorable sites for a new geothermical installation

In this second part of the study, GIS is used to cross the data concerning the resource with other demographic, tectonic and surface data in order to determine the most favorable zones for a geothermic exploitation.

4.1 Criteria

It has been decided than the best location areas are the areas matching the following criteria:

- Zones with high resources potential and low access cost (determined in the first part of the study).

- Zones where a good transmissivity is possible. It is assumed that faulted zones are more permeable, and therefore more interesting from this point of view.
- Zones where there can be a good heat / electricity conversion factor. It was shown by (Köhler, 2002) that the cooling vector of the surface cycle is a major parameter. The refrigeration through water leads to conversion factors clearly much higher than refrigeration through ambient air. The presence of large water streams at the surface is therefore an asset for the installation of a power plant.
- Zones with a high demand of electricity, but especially of heat in surface. It is possible to have two income sources: by electricity sale, but also by heat sale. It was difficult to find geo-referenced data on heat networks. The choice was thus not limited to zones supplied by heat networks, but to zones in which potential consumers of heat (urban and industrial zones) are located. The heat network could indeed be specifically created for the geothermic installation.

4.2 Data sets

Resources: The resources location was the object of the first part of the study. In this first approach, only the potential has been evaluated. However, it was found that high potential was mainly found in deep zones, inducing a high drilling cost. In order to find a compromise between the available resources and the access cost to this one, it has been decided to keep only the zones where the extractable power is superior to 75 W by m depth of the aquifer. This value is completely subjective; it corresponds to the extracted resources of an aquifer of 170 °C situated to a depth of 3000 m, with a flow of 10 l/s. A more specific and detailed cost study would be necessary in order to validate or modify this value.

Faults: In order to be able to extract a lot of heat from the underground, it is important that the deep reservoir, working as a heat exchanger, have a surface as big as possible. For this reason, the faulted zones are interesting, they allow an important circulation of fluids. Data used have been digitized from paper maps provided by BRGM. The areas located within 1 km from big faults are therefore considered as very favorable areas.

Water streams: The water streams allow effective cooling of a geothermic facility, thus increasing the heat / electricity conversion factor (in comparison with a cooling using ambient air). Zones located in the proximity of a water stream (principally of important rivers) are more interesting for our aim.

For this part the CORINE (CoORdination of INformation on the Environment) database has been used. This Land Cover database includes water streams classified in three classes according to the width of the river.

Only large water streams have enough flow to cool a geothermal plant : areas located within 500 m from a water stream which is more than 15 m wide were considered.

Industrial and urban areas: These zones are interesting from an economical point of view, since they are potentially the energy demanding and consuming zones.

The CORINE data have been also utilized in this part. In this database, urban and industrial zones are two separated classes. These two information were grouped in the same layer in order to be used as fourth criteria.

4.3 Result

To complete the multi criteria approach, the four vector layers representing zones matching the four previous criteria are intersected. The resulting favorable zones for a geothermic facility are shown in Figure. 4.

Figure 4: Alsace map showing most favorable zones for a geothermic installation in Alsace

5 Results and discussion

From the first part of the study, we pointed out that the biggest resources are stored in the Buntsandstein aquifer. Two reasons can account for this: (i) this aquifer is the thickest, (ii) but it is also the deepest and thus the hottest. However, if we consider the power that can be extracted economically, there are few differences between the Buntsandstein and the Muschelkalk.

The favorable zones for geothermal electricity production are identified: they are mainly situated in the north-eastern part of Alsace, and ultimately around Sélestat and in the region situated between Colmar and Mulhouse. It has to be noted that the high potential zones are the ones where the aquifers are deeper (thus the cost to access the resources is higher).

The evaluation of the brutto power of a plant fed by the aquifer has been made using values for the transmissivity of the aquifers that are very bad constrained in the study area. In order not to over-evaluate the results, a rather low value was used. Consequently, the brutto power calculated for the plants is quite low (under 400kW). It must however be emphasized that the brutto power of a plant is proportional to the brine pumping rate, which itself is almost proportional to transmissivity. If the actual local transmissivity is twice the value used for the calculations, the power of the plant will thus be almost twice. Moreover, the stimulation of hydrothermal reservoirs can increase their transmissivity by a factor of 2. It must then be kept in mind that the calculated power of the plant is a minimum.

From the second part of the study we observe that most favorable zones for a geothermic installation are again mainly situated in the north-eastern part of the Alsace, mainly around Strasbourg. The interest of this very restricted localization is to be able to study in detail the conditions of the favorable areas.

The described methodology was implemented in an ArcGIS-based application, with options to be translated and adapted to other areas and other data sources : the study presented here is now being extended to the other suitable French regions.

In order to evaluate more precisely the relevance of geothermics in France, other aspects have to be taken into account. In particular, the final cost of electricity is a criterion that can not be ignored : the total costs and the internal energy demand of a geothermal plant have then to be evaluated more precisely. Further work should then be directed towards integration of detailed costs analysis.

6 Conclusions

The motivation of the study was to assess the potential for geothermal electricity production in the French part of the Rhine Graben and the location of favourable sites for its exploitation. The results show that this potential is huge: a sustainable production of the whole reservoirs during 100 years would enable to produce more energy than is presently needed in Alsace. A total exploitation of the aquifers is not realistic: however, this study has shown the potential of geothermics in one of the favorable areas in France. This area is not unique: other basins or grabens contain deep, hot aquifers in France and in Europe (Haenel & Staroste, 1988; Hurter & Haenel, 2002).

Finally, it has been demonstrated the important contribution of GIS techniques for the study of renewable energies. GIS only can perform the required cross data analysis that involves the corresponding data sets.

7 Acknowledgements

The authors like to thank all people that contributed to this work by their constructive review and professional knowledge.

8 References

Gringarten A.C., 1978. *Reservoir lifetime and heat recovery factor in geothermal aquifers used for urban heating*. Pageoph 117 : 297-308.

Haenel R. and Staroste E., 1988. *Atlas of Geothermal Resources in the European Community, Austria and Switzerland*. Publication of the European Commission.

Hurter S. and Haenel R., 2002. *Atlas of Geothermal Resources in Europe*. Publication of the European Commission.

Jung R., Röhling S., Ochmann N., Rogge R., Schellschmidt R., Schulz R. and Thielemann T., 2002. *Abschätzung des technischen Potenzials der geothermischen Stromerzeugung und der geothermischen Kraft-Wärme-Kopplung in Deutschland*. BGR Bericht.

Kohl T., Andenmatten N. and Rybach L., 2003. *Geothermal Resource Mapping – Example from northern Switzerland. Geothermics* 32 : 721-732.

Köhler S., 2002. *Geothermischen getriebene Kraftwerke – Systembetrachtung und Prozessvergleich.* In: VDI Berichte 1703, VDI-GET (Ed.), *Geothermische Stromerzeugung, Stand der Technik und Perspektiven*, pp 71-84.

Laurent H., 1974. *Inventaire des possibilités géothermiques de la région de Strasbourg (67) entre Gerstheim et Gambsheim.* Rapport BRGM.

Walgenwitz F., Maget P., Tietze R. and Neeb I., 1979. *Synthèse géothermique du Fossé Rhénan Supérieur.* Rapport BRGM – GLBW.

CORINE database available in internet:
http://dataservice.eea.eu.int/atlas/viewdata/viewpub.asp?id=1

Economic evaluation of electricity production from wind energy in Germany

D. Möst, J. Rosen, O. Rentz, Institute for Industrial Production (IIP), Universität Karlsruhe (TH), Germany

ABSTRACT: Electricity production from wind energy is constantly gaining importance in Germany. Both the operational and economic consequences of its contribution to the electricity supply will be evaluated within this paper. In a first step the wind energy development during the last decades and the compensation schemes used in Germany will be described. The development of financing schemes for wind energy from an owner's perspective will be described starting with local citizens participation schemes up to closed-end funds. Afterwards, the wind energy will be analysed from an energy utility's perspective, which means especially the fact of providing fast adjustable power plants for balancing fluctuating wind energy and necessary grid extensions. Attention is also paid to the financial burden for final consumers through wind energy production. Finally, as externalities are not accounted for in the considerations, the conclusion is drawn that it would already today pay off to invest in renewable energies.

1 Introduction

The German Federal Government sees the Rio mandate[4] as an obligation. Through the national sustainability strategy, the formulation of which entails the broad-based involvement of society, the government is outlining its concrete ideas for the implementation of sustainable development, based on four key focal points – fairness to future generations, quality of life, social cohesion, and international responsibility. At the core of the national sustainability strategy are a number of long-term targets, designed to provide orientation for governments and social players, as well as a set of key indicators, including a number that reflect important environmental aspects of sustainable development. They help to describe environmental development and to highlight progress and trends by offering clear measurement variables. One of these indicators is the renewable energy sources indicator, i.e. the *proportion of renewable energy sources in primary energy consumption and electricity consumption.* Within this indicator the quantified ecological target is to increase the proportion of renewable energy sources to 4.2 % of primary energy consumption and to 12.5 % of electricity consumption by 2010 (doubling by 2010 compared to 2000 levels) (German Environmental Report, 2002).

To achieve this target, the government enacted the Erneuerbare-Energien-Gesetz (EEG, Act on Granting Priority to Renewable Energy Sources), which has lead to a construction of more than 15,000 wind power installations in the last 10 years in Germany. In opposition to this success story, mainly energy utilities in Germany state that wind energy burdens final consumers and the German business location. Through the continuous discussion on wind energy and the conflictive information, the electricity production from wind energy in Germany will be analysed in this paper. Especially the economic effects for energy utilities

[4] Mandate of the United Nations Framework Convention on Climate Change ratified at the United Nations Conference on Environment and Development in Rio de Janeiro in 1992

and investors in wind energy plants will be analysed. Before analysing the situation for these two players, an overview about wind energy in Germany will be given.

2 Wind Energy in Germany

The total electricity production in Germany in 2003 was about 560 TWh, whereof about 45 TWh have been produced from renewable energies (VDEW, 2004), which equals 8 %. The production of wind energy is growing steadily (cf. figure 1) and reached about 19 TWh in 2003, which equals about 3.4 % of the total production. The average utilisation of wind power installations was about 1300 full load hours.

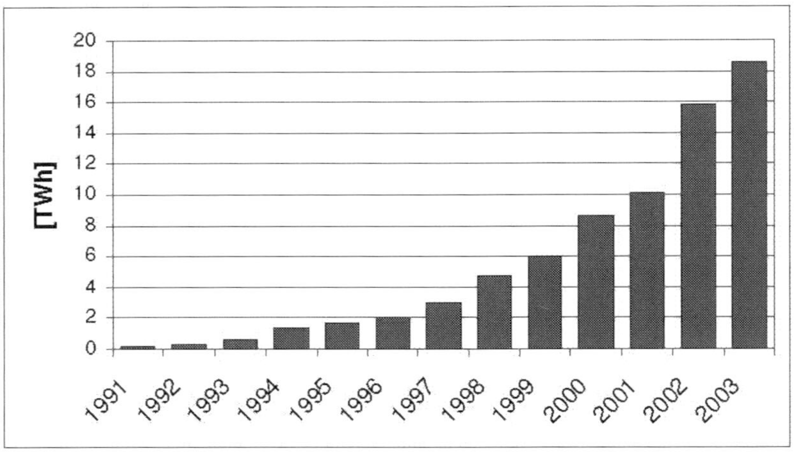

Figure 1: Electricity production from wind energy in Germany

The installed capacity of wind power in Germany reached about 16.6 GW in 2004, which is about 35 % of the world wide installed capacity (cf. table 1). The spatial distribution of wind energy plants in Germany shows that the majority of the wind turbines is installed in the northern part amounting approximately 9 GW. The two main reasons for this are higher average wind speeds in Northern Germany and little surface roughness due to a plain landscape. Thus, the installed capacity per area is extremely high in the northern part. Forecasts for the total installed capacity of wind energy plants state about 22 GW for 2010 and 43 GW for 2020 including offshore plants. Table 1 shows global wind power statistics.

Table 1: Global wind power statistics (Source: www.wwindea.org)

Country	Additional Capacity in 2004 [MW]	Rate of Growth in 2004 [%]	Total Capacity installed end 2004 [MW]	Country	Additional Capacity in 2004 [MW]	Rate of Growth in 2004 [%]	Total Capacity installed end 2004 [MW]
Germany	2,019	13.8	16,628	Sweden	43	10.8	442
Spain	2,061	33.2	8,263	France	138	55.6	386
USA	370	5.8	6,740	Australia	181	92.2	379
Denmark	7	0.2	3,117	Ireland	152	82.2	338.9
India	875	41.5	2,985	Egypt	120	66.7	300
Italy	221	24.4	1,125	Norway	176	176.0	276
The Netherlands	170	18.7	1,078	New Zealand	131	362.5	167
Japan	390	77.1	896	Belgium	27	39.7	95
United Kingdom	240	37.0	888	Finland	29	57.8	80
China	197	34.7	764	Costa Rica	0	0.0	79
Austria	191	46.0	606	Ukraine	12	21.6	68
Portugal	223	74.6	522	Korea	48	209.3	68.4
Greece	124	34.0	489	Poland	6	10.5	63
Canada	122	37.9	444	World	8,321	21.2	47,616

3 Compensation

The current version of the EEG came into force in 2004, displacing the former version of the EEG. On its part, it had taken the place of the Stromeinspeisegesetz (StrEG, law on payment for electrical supplies) in 2000, until then having built the basis for the feed-in of electricity produced from renewable energies. The calculation of the feed-in-tariff in the StrEG was based on a fixed percentage of the average revenues of the electric utilities and thus in no way cost-oriented. The compensation for renewable energies declined with the fall of the electricity prices in the liberalised market. With the introduction of the EEG replacing the StrEG renewable energies have grown steadily. Within the EEG, the compensation scheme is based on a country wide homogenous feed-in tariff and grid operators are obliged to connect renewable electricity generation installations to their grids, to purchase electricity available from these installations as a priority, and to compensate the suppliers of this electricity in accordance with the provisions. The EEG comprises compensations schemes for electricity generated from hydropower, wind power, biomass, geothermal energy, solar radiation energy, gas from landfill, mines, and sewage treatment plants. The amendment of the EEG in 2004 implicates modified compensation tariffs. It distinguishes, for instance, onshore and offshore wind energy plants and provides them with different tariffs, in the case of onshore wind energy plants with lower tariffs than before. Regarding electricity from biomass, geothermal, and solar electricity the compensation tariffs were raised.

Table 2: Compensation for electricity generated from renewables (EEG, 2004)

Technology	Feed-in tariff				Comments
Hydropower	9.67 ct/kWh (< 500 kW)		6.65 ct/kWh (< 5 MW)		Compensation restricted to 5 MW ceiling, annual degression of 1% for new plants from 1/1/2005 on
Landfill gas, coal bed methane and sewage gas installations	7.67 ct/kWh (< 500 kW)		6.65 ct/kWh (< 5 MW)		Compensation restricted to 5 MW ceiling, annual degression of 1.5% for new plants from 1/1/2005 on
Biomass	11.5 ct/kWh (< 150 kW)	9.9 ct/kWh (< 500 kW)	8.9 ct/kWh (< 5 MW)	8.4 ct/kWh (5 MW<x<20MW)	Compensation restricted to 20 MW ceiling, annual degression of 1.5% for new plants from 1/1/2005 on
Geothermal	15 ct/kWh (< 5MW)	14 ct/kWh (< 10 MW)	8.95 ct/kWh (< 20 MW)	7.16 ct/kWh (> 20MW)	Compensation not restricted, degression of 1% for new plants from 1/1/2010 on
Wind power	onshore		offshore		Onshore: period of higher tariff is prolonged for projects whose yields do not reach 150% of reference yield Offshore: higher tariff is paid if plant into operation until 31/12/2010.
	8.7 ct/kWh (first 5 years)	5.5 ct/kWh (remaining period)	9.1 ct/kWh (first 12 years)	6.19 ct/kWh (remaining period)	
Photovoltaics	57.4 ct/kWh (< 30 kW)	54.6 ct/kWh (> 30 kW)		54 ct/kWh (> 100 kW)	Values for plants on building or noise barrier Compensation increased by 5 ct/kW if plant not on roof and not serving as roof of building

For wind energy the compensation to be paid for electricity generated onshore shall be 8.7 Cent/kWh for a minimum period of 5 years in case of a project yield reaching 150 per cent of the yield of the reference plant. The compensation in the thereon following years depends on the electricity production in the first five years and shall be 5.5 Cent/kWh. From 1 January 2005 on for onshore plants and from 1 January 2008 on for offshore plants respectively, the minimum compensation amounts specified above are reduced by 2 % annually for new installations commissioned as of this date; the amounts payable are rounded to two decimal (cf. table 2).

4 Economic Evaluation of Electricity Production from wind energy

4.1 Developers' and Owners' Perspective

Before evaluating the situation for wind energy plants, the certain aspects, such as the legal form, financing scheme and ownership, will be described.

At the beginning of the wind energy development in Germany in the 80ies, there were motivated private auto-producers driven by ecological concerns starting to run wind energy turbines of small or medium wind energy capacities. Generation output has been used to, at least partially, satisfy own consumption. With the growth in turbine size and thereby also in investment, private persons were no longer able to finance a wind energy installation on their own. So the Bürgerwindparks came up, a participation scheme where local citizens formed a group of interested "green energy producers", who developed and financed the wind energy projects. With further development of the wind turbines, this participation scheme with local citizens got more and more professional. With the separation of project development and financing, the today's market maturity in the wind energy business has been reached. Nowadays, professional green independent power producers develop projects; whereas investment and plant operation is profit-driven and all generated output is supplied to the grid. The equity capital of these wind installations, which mainly form part of larger wind parks, is typically derived from project shares that are offered at the finance market as financial products similar to closed-end ship or property funds. The former Bürgerwindparks and the closed-end fund structure are principally based on the same legal form of a private limited liability company and a limited partnership (GmbH & Co. KG).

The market volume of such wind funds in Germany has reached 432m € equity capital in 2002, with an average equity share of 30 %. Loan capital nearly exclusively derives from three sources: "ERP – Umwelt- und Energiesparprogramm" (European Recovery Program: Environment and Energy Saving Program), the DtA-Umweltprogramm (Deutsche Ausgleichsbank: Environment Program) and the KfW (Kreditanstalt für Wiederaufbau).

The compensation scheme described above has two main advantages for project developers, which lead to this enormous growth within the renewable energy business. Each energy project is exposed to a characteristic set of project risks comprising commercial, technical, and other risks, with the latter to also be expressed commercially in the end. One of the main commercial risks is the market risk of the electricity sale, implying price uncertainty on the one hand and the future sales volume on the other - not to mistake with the risk of production volume. But both risks have been smoothed out for the project developer by the new EEG-law. There is no price uncertainty, because a fixed feed-in tariff is guaranteed and further more, there is no risk on the sales volume, due to the fact that grid operators are obliged to purchase electricity available from these installations as a priority.

Due to the fact, that even the first developed wind farms did not reach the end of the total project duration, only prospected cash flow calculations can be considered for profitability calculations. However, given that there is still little experience in the marketplace regarding real cost developments after several years of operation, any profitability projection still includes significant uncertainties. Projected rates of return typically range between 7 and 9 %, excluding tax advantages.

4.2 Energy Utilities' Perspective

Energy utilities are obliged to ensure the security of electricity supply. Contrary to conventional and also some renewable electricity sources, wind energy cannot be scheduled and problems can arise for the grid, the operation and the structure of the conventional plant portfolio, especially in regions with high wind power capacities. Due to the fluctuations of wind energy, utilities have to provide fast adjustable power plants for balancing power. A number of issues and disadvantages arise for energy utilities and grid operators (described e.g. in dena, 2005), which have to be taken care of:

- More extreme load situations are faced in the grid, necessitating grid extensions.

- Installed capacities of wind energy plants contribute to the secured capacity of the plant portfolio only to a small degree, which decreases with wind power penetration, i.e. more reserve capacities are needed.
- The less predictable residual load curve requires more frequent start-up procedures of conventional power stations and causes a decreasing efficiency due to more frequent partial load operation (higher specific fuel consumption) and due to the increasing provision of balancing power necessary.
- Average production costs in the conventional plant portfolio rise (passed on to consumers as rising prices on the competitive market) as workload decreases due to the required higher flexibility of power plants and the necessary reserve capacities.

As electricity production from wind power depends on the volatile wind supply, only a small share of installed capacities of wind energy plants can add to the **secured capacities** within a conventional-renewable plant portfolio. Additionally, the specific secured capacities diminish with a rising share of wind power. The gain in secured capacity depends on seasonal variations due to changing wind conditions from season to season as displayed in table 3.

Table 3: Seasonal gain in secured capacities of wind energy plants per MW of installed wind power capacity (Bartels et al., 2005)

	2003	2007	2010	2015
	In % of installed wind power capacity			
Winter	8.3	6.9	6.5	6.0
Spring	8.6	7.2	6.9	6.4
Summer	6.1	5.3	5.4	5.1
Autumn	7.2	6.1	5.9	5.5

Possible forecast errors of wind energy feed-in require **additional balancing energy and reserve power** and raise the demand for balancing and reserve energy. Although an improving forecast quality can be assumed for future years, the rising share of installed wind power will bring about a disproportionately high increase of demand for balancing and reserve power. It is assumed that in 2015 an additional 7.064 MW of positive balancing and reserve power will have to be provided for (see table 4), as well as an additional 5.6 TWh/a of positive balancing energy, compared to 2.1 TWh/a in 2003.

There are three main reasons for rising electricity costs. In the first place the integration of wind power into the conventional plant portfolio causes changes as the workload of conventional power plants decreases and therefore **rising average production costs**. Secondly, as the integration requires rising provision and demand of positive and negative balancing power, the prices on the balancing energy market rise causing on their part an **increase of prices on the competitive market**.

The costs for the onshore **extension of the extra high voltage transmission grid** are estimated to amount to about 0.28 billion Euros up to the year 2007, approximately 0.49 billion Euros for the period 2007 to 2010, and from the years 2010 to 2015 about 0.35 Euros. The grid connection of offshore plants will cost approximately 5 billion Euros up to the year 2015. Up to the year 2015 the fees for grid use will rise by 0.025 Cent/kWh.

Table 4 Additional demand for balancing and reserve capacities in dependency of installed wind power capacity (Bartels et al., 2005)

	2003	2007	2010	2015
	Additional positive need for balancing and reserve capacity in MW			
Maximum	2,077	4,089	5,534	7,064
To be contracted 'day ahead' (mean)[5]	1,178	2,094	2,623	3,227
	Additional negative need for balancing and reserve capacity in MW			
Maximum	1,871	3,429	4,304	5,480
To be contracted 'day ahead' (mean)[2]	753	1,396	2,020	2,822

As already mentioned, the additional generation capacity of newly installed wind projects has a very limited added capacity value for the overall supply system, all the more in that today's European energy situation is characterised by existing overcapacities. Only in the long term further generation capacities are needed. Consequently, only fuel costs and variable costs of replaced plants in operation can be avoided in the short term. These avoided electricity supply costs depend on the replaced mix of power plants. Based on full costs, the Federal Ministry for the Environment, Nature Conservation and Nuclear Safety estimates these avoided electricity supply costs for the year 2005 to be at about 4.3 Cent/kWh and the avoided CO_2 emissions at 800 g CO_2/kWh (BMU, 2002) without taking efficiency losses into account.

Own calculations at IIP based on a short-term power plant scheduling model and taking efficiency losses into account lead to 1.4 Cent/kWh of avoided fuel and variable costs and 650 g CO_2/kWh of avoided emissions. The short-term model aims at simulating interdependencies between increasing amounts of fluctuating electricity production, especially wind power, and the operation of the conventional plant portfolio. The input provided to the short-term model consists of interpolated load curves, data of the future energy system structure established by a long-term optimising power system model[6] and the feed-in of renewable electricity. Special consideration is given to data sets to be chosen representing average wind years or ones above and below average. As the numbers given above indicate the model can be used to quantify the effects and the actual (net) benefits of wind power feed-in in terms of costs and emissions. To give an example of how the model is calculated with, the power plant portfolio installed in Germany in the year 2000 and the electricity demand are be taken as a reference. Furthermore wind power is introduced at three different stages of capacities, such as 6 GW in 2000, 17.3 GW in 2005 and 22.4 GW in 2010, producing 12, 34.9 and 50.9 TWh respectively. The results indicate that mainly coal-fired plants will be replaced by wind energy. They also show that the amount of gas-fired electricity displaced is negligible and even decreases for higher shares of wind energy, as gas-fired plants are needed to compensate for the short-term fluctuations of wind power.

[5] Demand for balancing and reserve power is calculated from the day-ahead forecasted level of wind energy feed-in.

[6] For these calculations the long-term optimising energy system model PERSEUS (Program package for emission reduction strategies in energy use and supply) was used. A detailed description of the PERSEUS model can be found in (Enzensberger, 2003)

In order to quantify the effects of wind energy in the long term, several framework conditions like primary energy prices, emission ceilings, and the German case of nuclear energy phase-out have to be considered. Model results of the long-term optimising power system model developed at IIP mentioned above show, that wind energy substitutes hard coal power plants and partially the construction of new gas-fired combined cycle power plants, if the wind energy production is given as a model input. Consequently, the avoided electricity supply costs are higher than in the short term and amount to 3 Cent/kWh as a result of our calculations for the year 2005.

5 Financial burden for final consumers through wind energy

Due to the regulations of the EEG the feed-in tariffs to be paid for electricity generated from wind energy will be split up among all final consumers of electricity in Germany. Considering the electricity production from wind energy in 2000 (about 8.6 TWh) and the electricity delivered to final consumers in 2000 (about 500 TWh) this would lead to an average financial burden due to feed-in tariffs of about 0.11 Cent/kWh not considering the value of the electricity replaced by wind. Due to the estimated increase of electricity production from wind energy converters onshore and offshore (bei, 2002) and the slight increase of electricity delivered to final consumers this burden could rise to about 0.7 Eurocent per kWh in 2020. To calculate the net additional costs of wind energy feed-in the production costs per kWh of the electricity replaced have to be considered. Taking the above calculated avoided electricity supply costs into account, the estimates lead to additional costs of 0.11 Cent/kWh in 2000 and 0.40 Cent/kWh in 2010 (see Table 5).

Table 5: Financial burden through wind electricity production[7]

	2000	2005	2010
Electricity from wind energy [TWh]	8.6	22.5	30.4
Avoided electricity costs [Cent/kWh]	1.41	1.7	1.3
Financial burden for final consumers due to EEG-feed-in tariff (based on 500 TWh) [Cent/kWh]	0.11	0.28	0.40

The increase of consumers' prices has also been calculated for the dena-Netzstudie (cf. dena, 2005) and the results have been summarised (Bartels et al., 2005). They are displayed in Table 6 showing the rise of consumer prices for privileged and non-privileged consumers.

[7] An average feed-in tariff of 7.8 Cent/kWh for onshore power plant, synthesised from values of different sites is assumed, i.e. 6.63 Cent/kWh for very good wind sites, 8.24 Cent/kWh for average wind sites, and 8.53 Cent/kWh for less favourable wind sites. All values are assumed for 20 years of operation (BWE, 2005).

Table 6: Rise of consumer prices (Bartels et al., 2005)

	2007	2010	2015	2007	2010	2015
	in €(2003)/MWh					
	Non-privileged consumer			Privileged consumer		
Basis scenario[8]	1.6	4.4	4.6	0.4	1.8	1.5
Basis scenario + CO_2[9]	1.5	3.2	3.9	0.4	1.0	1.5
Alternative scenario	1.4	3.5	3.6	0.3	1.5	1.5

6 Summary and Conclusion

In this paper the structural, operational, and economic effects of wind power production in Germany have been portrayed. Further, the contribution of wind power to electricity supply during the last decade has been evaluated from the perspectives of both wind park owners (compensation, legal forms) and utilities (grid issues, reserve capacities, balancing power).

Finally, also the financial burden for final consumers through wind energy production has been quantified. It should be kept in mind that within the calculations and results shown above, externalities are not accounted for by the producers and consumers of energy, i.e. they are not included in the market prices. Externalities include damage to the natural and built environment, such as effects of air pollution on health, buildings, crops, forests, and global warming, as well as occupational diseases and accidents, reduced amenity from visual intrusion of plants or emissions of noise. The traditional economic assessment of fuel cycles has tended to ignore these effects. However, there is a growing interest in adopting a more sophisticated approach involving the quantification of these environmental and health impacts of energy use and their related external costs (cf. Fleury et al., 2004). There are a lot of uncertainties and problems connected to the identification, quantification and monetary evaluation of externalities. Within the ExternE studies (cf. e.g. European Commission, 1999), the external costs for wind energy are quantified to be between 0.04 and 0.22 Cent/kWh compared to 1.7 to 17 Cent/kWh for coal-fired plants. (Krewitt & Nitsch, 2002) reason that costs for the feed-in of renewable energies by the EEG will be compensated by avoided damages caused to the environment. Furthermore, wind energy reduces the dependency of fuel imports and thus is able to improve the security of supply. Hence, taking these considerations into account, it does already today pay off to invest in wind energy and other renewable energies.

7 References

Bartels, M., C. Gatzen, M. Peek, and R. Wissen. 2005. *Auswirkungen des Windenergie-ausbaus auf Struktur und Kosten der Stromerzeugung in Deutschland - Ergebnisse der dena-Netzstudie*. ZfE Zeitschrift für Energiewirtschaft 29(1):3-10.

[8] Assumptions: moderate rise in gas, oil and coal price, and a constant lignite price; price for CO_2 certificates do not influence cost and price calculations of companies.

[9] Assumptions: same price development for fossil fuels as reference scenario; CO_2 certificates price assumptions: 2007 €5 Euro/t CO_2, 2010 €10/t CO_2, 2015 €12.5 /t CO_2; influence on cost and price calculations of companies

bei. bremer energie institut. 2002. Windenergienutzung und zukünftige Entwicklung des Kraftwerkparks in Deutschland. Bremen, 2002.

BMU. 2002. *German Environmental Report*. Federal Ministry for the Environment, Nature Conservation and Nuclear Safety, www.bmu.de.

BWE. 2005. *Vergütung für Strom aus Windenergie*. www.wind-energie.de/index.php?id=264

dena. 2005. *Energiewirtschaftliche Planung für die Netzintegration von Windenergie in Deutschland an Land und Offshore bis zum Jahr 2020*. On behalf of the German Energy Agendy (dena). Final Report. Köln, 2005.

EEG. 2004. *Gesetz für den Vorrang Erneuerbarer Energien*. BGBl. Teil I Nr. 40, 31.07.2004.

Enzensberger, N. *Entwicklung und Anwendung eines Strom- und Zertifikatsmarktmodells für den europäischen Energiesektor*, VDI-Fortschritts-Berichte, Reihe 16, Nr. 159, VDI Verlag Düsseldorf, 2003

European Commission. 1999. DGXII, Science, Research and Development. Externalities of Fuel Cycles. ExternE Project, Report Nr. 7 Methodology 2nd ed., 1999.

Fleury, A., W. Fichtner, and O. Rentz. 2004. *Energy System Analysis Models for Sustainable Energy Production*. In International Conference on Sustainable Indicators and Intelligent Decisions (SIID). Vilnius, 2004.

Krewitt, W., and J. Nitsch. 2002. *Das EEG – eine Investition zahlt sich schon heute aus*. Energiewirtschaftliche Tagesfragen, Heft 7, 2002.

Rosen, J., D. Möst, W. Fichter, and O. Rentz. 2003. *Use of the PERSEUS models to analyse the effects of large-scale renewable energy production*. Proceedings of the 17th International Conference Informatics for Environmental Protection (EnviroInfo) 2003, Cottbus

VDEW. 2004. www.vdew.de.

Evaluation of renewable promotion schemes in the European Electricity market

Anne Held, Mario Ragwitz, Martin Wietschel, Fraunhofer Institute for Systems and Innovation Research, Karlsruhe, Germany

ABSTRACT: Since the publication of the White Paper "Energy for the future" and the adoption of the Directive 2001/77/EC on renewable energies in the electricity sector, the EU renewable energy sector has developed in a dynamic way. All member states have introduced policies to support the market introduction of renewable electricity. This study aims to assess existing renewable support mechanisms with a focus on the currently dominant feed-in tariffs and quota obligations in combination with tradable green certificates. Using case studies, both the coherence of effectiveness and economic efficiency are investigated for wind energy in selected member states of the European Union. As a general conclusion it can be stated that the investigated feed-in systems are effective at relatively high economic efficiency. On the other hand it can be observed that in the present status quota systems reach only a rather low effectiveness at comparably low economic efficiency. However, these quota systems are rather new instruments in all countries which are currently using them. Therefore, the observed behaviour might still be characterised by significant transient effects.

1 Introduction

1.1 Background

Since renewable energy sources (RES) contribute to climate protection and the security of electricity supply in Europe, increasing the share of RES was cited as an essential objective in the White paper "Energy for the future: Renewable sources of energy" (1997). The member states of the European Union were requested to stipulate national indicative targets in order to provide 21% of the total electricity consumption in the EU-25 using RES by the year 2010 (European Parliament, Council of the European Union 2001). Although RES have become considerably more important in recent years, there remains a substantial development potential. Because of the comparatively high electricity generation costs of RES, the market development up to now has been supported by various policy promotion schemes. However, the application of such schemes usually implies a financial burden for the national economies. As a consequence, the currently applied RES promotion schemes need to be critically reviewed.

1.2 Objective and Methodology

At the moment, the discussion about how to optimally promote renewable energy focuses on the comparison of feed-in tariffs and quota obligations in combination with tradable green certificates. Hence, this study assesses these promotion schemes as well as further support schemes like tender procedures, investment support and fiscal incentives. An important objective is the identification of the most appropriate portfolio of policy instruments to promote renewable energy. Therefore, reliable criteria have to be defined to assess the success of support schemes. This study suggests a possible approach to evaluate policy instruments taking into account the impacts made on the capacity growth of renewable energies in correlation with economic efficiency. As the market development of renewable energy sources is heavily dependent on potential investors' decisions whether to realize investments or not, the economic efficiency is evaluated from an investor's perspective. Therefore, time-adjusted methods of investment analysis were used to calculate the expected annuity of investments in wind energy. The applied approach considers the financial support offered by the policy instruments over the whole lifetime of the plant. Finally, the results of the correlation between the expected annuity and the effectiveness are interpreted as regards the role of the different kinds of policy schemes.

2 Policy support schemes implemented in Europe

At present, the system of fixed **feed-in tariffs** is the dominant policy scheme for promoting electricity generation with RES in Europe. This system allows electricity generators to sell electricity using renewables at a fixed tariff for a determined period of time. Feed-in tariffs are currently implemented in Austria, Denmark (transitional regulation), France, Germany, Greece, Luxembourg, the Netherlands, Portugal and Spain. The feed-in tariff is price based, i.e. the quantity of electricity generation is determined by the market based on the set price (Haas et al., 2004).

Recently, some European countries like Belgium, Italy, Sweden, the UK and Poland have replaced the existing policy instruments with a **quota obligation**. The basic principle of this system is the determination of an obligation for consumers, suppliers or producers to provide a certain percentage of the electricity using RES. Generally, quota obligations are implemented in combination with tradable green certificates. The revenue from selling green electricity comprises the market electricity price as well as the value of the green certificates. Since the certificate price depends on the predefined target and is determined on the market, the quota obligation combined with tradable green certificates constitutes a quantity-based approach(Haas et al., 2004).

In addition, RES can be promoted by the quantity-based **tender scheme**, which was formerly applied in the United Kingdom and is still being used in Ireland and France. However, Ireland plans to replace its tender scheme by feed-in tariffs. The essential component of a tender scheme is a bidding round including a competition for financial support conceded to projects with the lowest generation costs (International Energy Agency [IEA], 2004, S. 87).

Other existing policy schemes to promote renewable energy include **fiscal incentives** and **investment grants**. Fiscal incentives either offer a tax reduction or exemption to producers of renewable electricity or reduce the taxable income. Thus, the supporting effect of fiscal incentives stems from reduced expenditure rather than additional revenues. Investment grants can be used to lower the capital costs of investing in RES and thus also the investor's risk. Fiscal incentives as well as investment grants are often applied in combination with other policy schemes in order to provide extra support.

Table 1 gives an overview of the RES-E support schemes described

Table 1: Classification of policy measures to support renewable energy

Price-based mechanisms	Quantity-based mechanisms
• Feed-in tariffs • Fiscal incentives • Investment grants	• Quota obligation in combination with tradable green certificates • Tender schemes

3 Criteria of evaluation

3.1 Effectiveness

The effectiveness is one criterion to analyse the different policy schemes promoting renewable electricity. In this study it is measured by an indicator which contains the increase in the electricity generation potential compared to a suitable reference quantity. The electricity generation potential represents the electricity output potential of all the plants installed up to the end of each year. Generally, the electricity generation potential is determined by the product of the installed capacity and the fixed amount of full load hours per year. Since policy instruments do not have any influence on electricity output volatility due to the weather, the generation potential was preferred to the actual electricity output. Moreover, the additional available renewable electricity generation potential was chosen as the reference quantity. This additional mid-term potential describes the theoretically realisable electricity generation until the year 2020 considering the country and the technology specific framework involved[10]. The effectiveness of a policy scheme is defined as the ratio of the change of the electricity generation potential during a given period of time and the additional realisable mid-term potential until 2020. The exact definition of effectiveness is given in formula (1).

$$E = \frac{Q_{t+x} - Q_t}{x} * \frac{1}{(P_t^{2020} - Q_t)}$$

E = Effectiveness indicator; t = Start year of the period under consideration; (1)
x = Period under consideration; Q = Existing electricity generation potential;
P_t^{2020} *= Additional realisable midterm potential in t until* 2020

This definition of effectiveness has the advantage of being unbiased with regard to the available potential for individual technologies in a specific country. Member states need to develop specific RES proportionally to the given potential to demonstrate the comparable effectiveness of their instruments. This appears to be a meaningful approach since the member state targets, as determined in the Directive 2001/77/EC, are also derived based mainly on the realisable generation potential of each country.

[10] The additional mid-term potential was determined in the project "Green-X", which analysed different strategies for the promotion of renewable energies in a dynamic context (c. p. Ragwitz et al., 2003).

3.2 Economic Efficiency

When assessing the economic efficiency of the support schemes, it is inadequate to only consider the current support level, since relevant design criteria like the duration of support or the future development of the financial support level are not taken into account. For instance, feed-in tariffs may include a degression of the tariffs during the validity period of the support or quota obligations may allow green certificates trading only for a determined period of time. Furthermore, the support level should be adapted to the actual conditions in the different countries, for example, differing expenditure have to be considered. In the case of wind energy, there are different electricity generation costs due to local wind conditions. The most important factor influencing the effectiveness of support schemes is the stimulation of investments in renewable energy projects. Thus, investments in renewable energy have to be made attractive to potential investors. Time-adjusted methods of investment analyses represent a possible approach for assessing economic efficiency. Accordingly, the annual average profit over the entire lifetime is used as an efficiency indicator. The annuity calculates the specific discounted average return on every sold energy unit by taking into account income and expenditure throughout the entire lifetime of a technology. It is defined in formula (2).

$$A = \sum_{t=0}^{n} \frac{(I_t - E_t)}{(1+i)^t} * \frac{(1+i)^n * i}{(1+i)^n - 1} \qquad (2)$$

$A = Annuity;\quad I_t = Income\ in\ t;\quad E_t = Expenditure\ in\ t;\quad i = Interest\ rate;\quad n = Lifetime$

Assumptions

The average expected annuity of wind energy investments for Germany, Spain, France, Austria, Belgium, Italy, Sweden, the UK, Ireland and Finland was calculated based on the expected support level during the period the promotion is given. Germany, Spain, France[11] and Austria represent countries with a feed-in tariff system, whereas Belgium, Italy, Sweden and the UK use quota obligations with certificate trading to promote renewable energy. Currently, Ireland applies tender procedures, although a switch to feed-in tariffs is planned. The promotion of RES in Finland is done using investment grants and tax exemptions.

Income and Expenditure

Concerning the countries with **feed-in tariffs**, the annual income is represented by tariffs paid for the green electricity determined by the corresponding law[12]. The level of support in the German system is annually adjusted according to the degression in the German Renewable Energy Act (EEG). Spain provides a market-oriented alternative in addition to a common fixed price system, which offers a premium payment for producers actuating on the national electricity market. The total income from the market option is larger than the fixed price option in order to stimulate green electricity participation on the market. Whereas the support duration in Germany and Spain is guaranteed for 20 years, French green electricity producers can anticipate 15 years of financial support, and in Austria, tariffs are guaranteed for 13 years.

For the four countries using quota obligation systems, the **certificate prices** of the year 2004 were assumed to remain constant for the entire active period of the support. This assumption

[11] France applies feed-in tariffs for plants < 12 MW and tender procedures for plants > 12 MW.

[12] Bundesministerium für Umwelt, Naturschutz und Reaktorsicherheit [BMU] 2000; IG Windkraft 2005; Ministère de l'Économie, des Finances et de l'Industrie 2001; Ministerio de Industria y Energía 2004

might be questionable because certificate prices might relax as the certificate markets in those countries mature. However, only very little knowledge exists about the temporal development of prices in these markets. In Belgium it is possible to participate in green certificate trading for 10 years, in Italy for 8. It also has to be mentioned that different systems are applied in the different regions of Belgium, i.e. in Flanders, Wallonia and Brussels. This study only examined the quota system used in Flanders and Wallonia because certificate trading did not take place in 2004. With regard to Sweden and the UK, it is assumed that participation can take place throughout the entire lifetime of the wind power plants.

In Finland, the financial support consists of **incentives** of 40% of total **investment** (Ragwitz et al. 2004). The **tax exemptions** conceded are also taken into account as additional income in order to include the tax effect in the investment analysis. In the UK as well as in Sweden, the tax exemption effect was considered in the same manner.

With regard to the **expenditure** incurred, country-specific prices were used according to the average market prices of wind turbines in 2004. To take country-specific wind resources into account, differing **full-load hours** were assumed.

Further parameters of investment analysis

The **lifetime** of the wind power plants was assumed to be 20 years for all the analysed countries. Generally, an **interest rate** of 6.6% was assumed for all countries except for Germany where an interest rate of 4.8% was used based on soft loans granted there which reduce the capital costs of the investment. The analysis was carried out for a hypothetical investment in wind onshore energy in the year 2003, with plant operation starting in 2004. Furthermore, the resulting series of payments were inflation-adjusted to the base year 2003 assuming an **inflation rate** of 1.3%.

4 Results

4.1 Effectiveness

Figure 1 shows the average annual effectiveness indicator for **wind onshore** electricity generation for the years 1997-2004 for the EU-15 and the EU-10 countries, respectively. Since significant policy changes came into effect in most EU member states during this period, the different support instruments applied in each country are shown in Figure 1. The most important policy changes are also described. Belgium, Sweden and the UK changed to quota systems based on tradable green certificates during 2002 or later. Therefore, a policy mix is considered in Belgium, France, Italy, the Netherlands, Sweden and the UK for the analysed period from 1997 to 2004.

Several messages can be derived from this figure. Firstly, the three member states Demark, Germany, and Spain, which have the highest effectiveness during the analysed period, all applied fixed feed-in tariffs during the entire period 1997-2004 (with a relevant system change in Denmark in 2001). So far, the use of feed-in tariffs has brought about an increase in the share of RES, amongst others due to the low investor risks involved and the long-term certainty concerning the guaranteed tariff level. However, as can be observed in a country like France, high administrative barriers can significantly hamper the development of wind energy even under a stable policy environment combined with reasonably high feed-in tariffs.

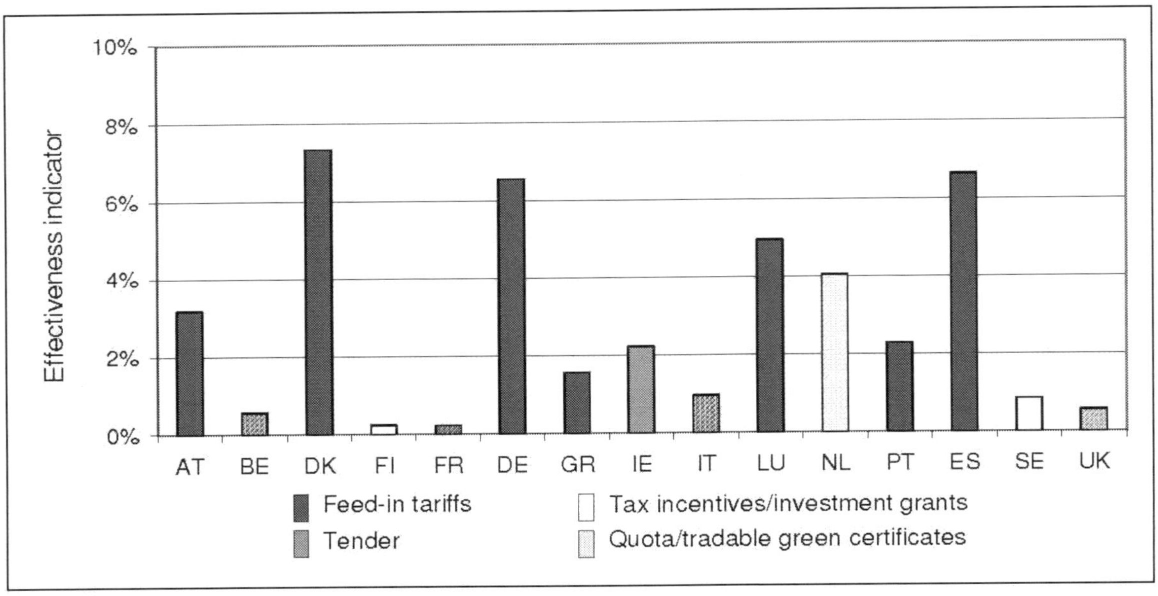

Figure 1: Effectiveness indicator for the existing electricity generation potential (wind onshore) in the period 1997-2004(Ragwitz et al. 2005). Diagonal shading indicates a switch of policy instruments in this period.

The evolution of the effectiveness indicator over time is shown in Figure 2 for selected member states of the EU-15.

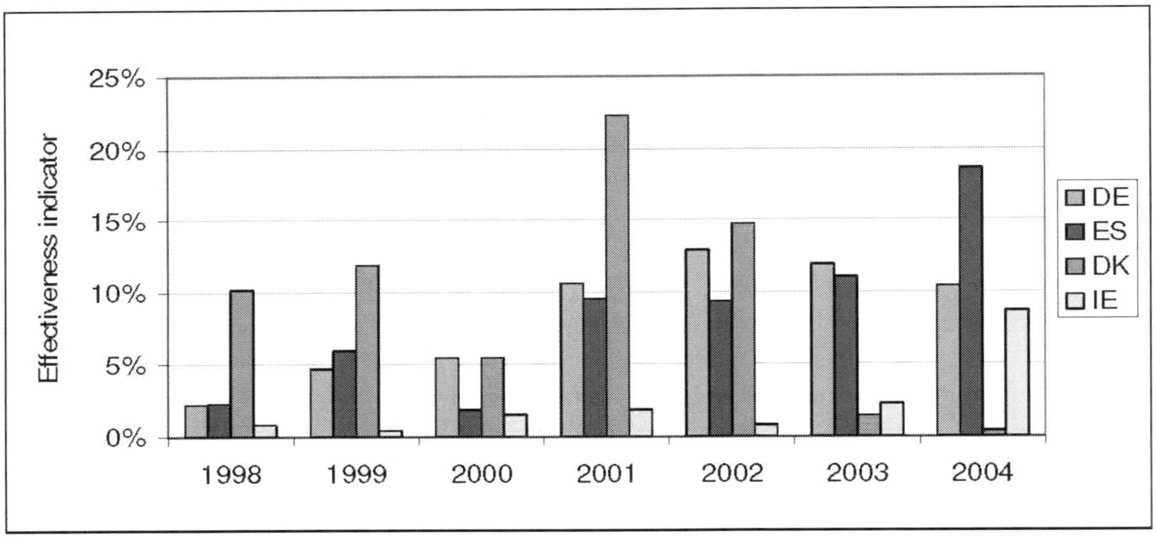

Figure 2: Evolution of the effectiveness indicator in Germany, Spain, Denmark and Ireland for wind onshore from 1998 to 2004(Ragwitz et al., 2005)

Regarding the evolution of effectiveness, it can be seen that Spain shows increasing effectiveness over time, whereas the Danish development underwent a sudden decline in 2003. In Germany, the effectiveness rose until 2002 and then decreased slightly due to a dearth in locations with good wind conditions. Figure 2 thus supports the view that a long-term and stable policy environment is a key criterion for the successful development of RES markets. For Ireland, the abrupt increase in 2004 stands out, which is a result of the recent bidding round in 2003.

4.2 Effectiveness versus economic efficiency

The results of the correlation between effectiveness and economic efficiency are illustrated in Figure 3. The indicator for economic efficiency is the annual expected profit from an investment in wind onshore energy.

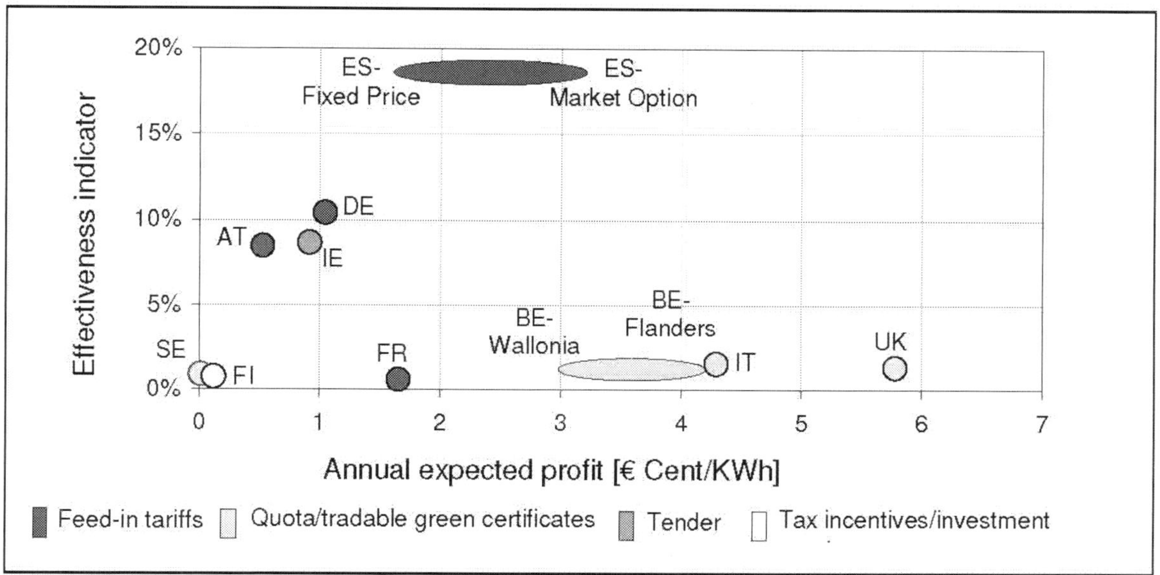

Figure 3: Effectiveness indicator versus the annual expected profit of an investment in wind onshore (Own calculations based on Ragwitz et al., 2005)

In Figure 3, the expected annuity as well as the effectiveness shows a broad spectrum in quantitative terms for the countries under consideration. It should be pointed out that the different instruments have different levels of maturity and that policy schemes in some countries - in particular quota obligation systems - are still in a transitional period. It is striking that **Italy**, the **UK** and **Belgium**, which have recently transformed their markets using **quota systems** as the main support instrument, are characterised by **high expected annual profits**, but low **effectiveness**. The high annuity results in particular from the extrapolation of the presently observed certificate prices. Although this assumption is questionable, the results show that certificate systems can lead to high producer profits compensating high investment risks.

On the other hand, countries with **feed-in-tariffs** seem to be typically **more effective** at generally **moderate annual profits**. France is one exception to this pattern, where strong administrative barriers are preventing a rapid development of wind energy in spite of favourable feed-in tariffs. **Spain** achieved the **highest growth rates** in terms of effectiveness combined with an adequate profit. The higher expected profit in Spain than in the other feed-in countries is not due to a high support level, but rather to relatively low electricity generation costs as a result of good resource conditions on the one hand and low investment costs on the other.

In 2004, the **Irish tender system** reached a **high level of effectiveness** similar to countries with feed-in-tariffs like Germany and Austria despite the significantly lower absolute support level. That the expected profit is similar is because of the significantly better wind resources in Ireland (2600 full load hours per year have been assumed for the typical Irish location, the corresponding figure in Germany amounts to 1800). However, the high Irish growth rate in 2004 has to be considered carefully since the comparatively high capacity development in this year is due to the results of the last Irish bidding round, whereas the growth rate was much smaller in former years. A tender system seems to be an instrument which promotes rapid growth in a short period of time. In **Sweden, the low growth** of wind power is due to the **low expected profit**.

As a general conclusion it can be stated that the investigated feed-in systems are effective at a relatively low producer profit. On the other hand it can be observed that, at present, quota systems only have rather low effectiveness at comparably high profit margins. We would like to emphasise, however, that these quota systems are comparatively new instruments in all the countries using them. Therefore the observed behaviour might still be characterised by significant transient effects.

5 Summary and Conclusions

An evaluation of the different policy schemes used to support renewable energy was carried out taking into account effectiveness and economic efficiency. Economic efficiency was examined from the investors' perspective based on the expected annual profit from an investment in wind onshore energy.

In summary, it can be concluded that **quota obligations in combination with tradable green certificates** have not been able to stimulate the market development of wind energy in spite of the estimated annual profit of about 3 – 6 € Cent/kWh (with the exception of Sweden). One important reason for this failure is probably the uncertain future development of the certificate prices as well as the lack of experience with such support schemes. The currently high level of certificate prices may be due to the risk premiums required by investors for assuming the investment risks. Thus, the risk of a possibly decreasing certificate price is supposed to be compensated for by higher profit requirements.

Where **feed-in tariff** systems were concerned, an expected annual profit of about 0.5 – 3 € Cent/kWh was sufficient to obtain high policy effectiveness with the exception of France. The crucial factor here seems to be the planning security transmitted to potential investors, particularly if the feed-in tariffs are guaranteed for a long period. In addition, it is easy to adjust the support conditions to different requirements and an adequate support level can be determined, for instance, in the form of a stepped feed-in tariff depending on the wind conditions, or a tariff degression according to expected technology progress.

It was apparently possible to achieve rapid effects with **tender procedures** due to ambitious tender targets, although they have not been able to stimulate continuous capacity growth.

Tax exemptions and **investment grants** are currently only used in Finland as the main policy schemes to support renewable energy so that the assessment of these kinds of support mechanisms was limited. In Finland, it was not possible to stimulate the market development of wind onshore energy using only tax exemptions and investment grants.

As a general conclusion it can be stated, that the effectiveness of various support schemes largely depends on the maturity and the credibility of the system. A stable planning is important to create a sound investment climate and to lower social costs as a result of lower risk premium. Administrative barriers can have a significant impact on the effectiveness of an instrument and hamper the effectiveness of in principle very powerful policy schemes. A continuous policy – avoiding a stop and go nature – is important to create a stable growth of renewable energy sources.

6 References

Bundesministerium für Umwelt, Naturschutz und Reaktorsicherheit [BMU] (2000): *Gesetz für den Vorrang erneuerbarer Energien [EEG].*

European Commission (1997): *Energy for the future: renewable sources of energy - White Paper for a community strategy and action plan.* COM (1997) 599 final.

European Parliament; Council of the European Union (2001): *Directive 2001/77/EC of the European Parliament and of the Council of 27 September 2001 on the promotion of electricity produced from renewable energy sources in the internal electricity market.*

Haas, R.; Eichhammer, W.; Huber, C.; Langniß, O.; Lorenzoni, A.; Madlener, R.; Menanteau, P.; Morthorst, P.-E.; Martins, A.; Oniszk, A.; Schleich, J.; Smith, A.; Vass, Z.; Verbruggen, A. (2004): *How to promote renewable energy systems successfully and effectively.* In: Energy Policy, 32, S. 833-839.

IG Windkraft (2005): *Geschichte der Windkraft in Österreich.* Available at: http://www.igwindkraft.at/index.php?mdoc_id=1000499. Download: 02.05.2005.

International Energy Agency [IEA] (2004): *Renewable Energy - Market & Policy Trends in IEA Countrys*, Paris.

Ministère de l'Économie, des Finances et de l'Industrie (2001): *Arrêté fixant les conditions d'achat de l'électricité produite par les installations utilisant l'énergie mécanique du vent, telles que visées à l'article 2-2° du décret n° 2000-1196 du 6 décembre 2000.* Available at: http://www.enertrag.com/download/recht/arrete_francais.pdf. Download: 14.03.2005.

Ministerio de Industria y Energía (2004): *Real Decreto 436.*

Ragwitz, M.; Held, A.; Sensfuss, F.; Huber, C.; Resch, G.; Faber, T.; Coenraads, R.; Morotz, A.; Jensen, S.G.; Morthorst, P.E.; Konstantinaviciute, I.; Heyder, B. (2005): *OPTRES - Assessment and optimisation of renewable support schemes in the European electricity market.* Interim Report (Draft), DGTREN.

Ragwitz, M.; Huber, C.; Resch, G.; White, S. (2003): *Dynamic cost-resource curves.* Available at: http://www.green-x.at/downloads/WP1%20-%20Dynamic%20cost-resource%20curves%20(Green-X)(final%20draft%2009-2003).pdf. Download: 15.02.2005.

Ragwitz, M.; Schleich, J.; Huber, C.; Faber, T.; Voogt, M.; Ruijgrok, W.; Bodo, P. (2004): *FORRES 2020: Analysis of the renewable energy's evolution up to 2020.* Final Report, confidential, DGTREN (Tender Nr. TREN/D2/10-2002).

The evolution of biomass digestion technology in the Netherlands

Simona Negro, Marko P. Hekkert and Ruud Smits,
Utrecht University, Utrecht, The Netherlands

ABSTRACT: Since the 70's research on energy conversion technologies, such as biomass digestion, has been carried out in the Netherlands. However, after thirty years biomass digestion has not been implemented successfully on large-scale. The aim of this paper is to create insight in the underlying factors of this troublesome trajectory by applying the Functions of Innovation Systems framework. This results in clear understanding of the (lack of) activities that took place in the innovation system of biomass digestion and the role of government policy. The analysis provides several lessons to take into account when developing policies for the acceleration of the development and application of biomass energy.

1 Introduction

Since the energy crises in the seventies and the increased climate change awareness in the nineties, research was carried out to find alternative energy sources to replace fossil fuels. One of the most promising alternatives is biomass. The potential of biomass is estimated in long term scenarios to contribute about up to 1135 EJ/year (Hoogwijk, 2004). Biomass is a very diverse energy carrier with a multitude of potential sources and applications and it may be the main renewable energy alternative that could compete on large scale with fossil fuels. Even though the potential of biomass is clear, this does not imply that the implementation of biomass energy is easy. In the Netherlands for example realisation of the national goals regarding the use of biomass energy is far behind schedule. Therefore, in this paper we analyse the troublesome history of the development and application of a specific biomass conversion technology, i.e., biomass digestion, to learn lessons from the difficulties and problems that characterise this development during the last 30 years.

Therefore our main research question is

How can we explain the low diffusion of biomass digestion technology in The Netherlands?

From earlier studies on the transformation of the energy system we have learned that the success of a new technology is not (only) determined by technological characteristics but (also) by the social system that develops, diffuses, implements or rejects new biomass technologies (Jacobsson & Bergek, 2004). We label this social system as 'Technology Specific Innovation System (TSIS)' based on (Jacobsson & Bergek, 2004).

The conceptual starting point of this paper is that a well functioning innovation system greatly improves the chance that the technology in question will be widely diffused. However, what determines whether an innovation system functions well or not? In a recent stream of articles, of which a significant number in Energy Policy, it is brought forward that a number of activities are of great influence to this system functioning, see (Jacobsson & Johnson, 2000; Johnson & Jacobsson, 2001a; Jacobsson & Johnson, 2001b; Sagar & Holdren 2002; Foxon et al., 2005). These key activities are labelled as 'Functions of Innovation Systems'. In earlier empirical papers these Functions of Innovation Systems are successfully used to describe the dynamics of innovation system development and deliver explanations for technological progress and diffusion. However, most of these analyses lack a research design in which all relevant activities are mapped over time to create insight in the precise functional patterns. In this case study we apply a method called history event analysis[13] to create deeper insight in the dynamics of innovation systems and the influence on technology development and diffusion. This will result in a more complete and thorough analysis, that will go beyond previous historical descriptions, where not only the development of the socio-technical landscape and the impact of mismatched rule-sets will be included (Raven, 2004).

Therefore the aim of this paper is not only to learn lessons from the unsuccessful story of biomass digestion but also to test the Functions of Innovation Systems approach in applying it in an innovative and thorough manner to structure empirical work.

The paper is structured as follows. In chapter 2 an overview of the background of the System of Innovation approach and the System Functions concept will be given with a focus on the functions that will be used in this paper. In chapter 3 the methodology, the boundaries and the technical aspects will be described. In chapter 4 the event description of biomass digestion and in chapter 5 an analysis of the function fulfilment will be provided. Chapter 6 will conclude this paper.

2 Theory

The underlying theory of this paper focuses on the 'lock-in' of established systems and the difficulty that firms encounter when they want to bring a new technology to the market (Unruh, 2000; Unruh, 2002). It is argued in Unruh (2000) that "industrial economies have been locked into fossil fuel-based energy systems through a process of technological and institutional co-evolution driven by path-dependant increasing returns to scale." He calls this condition 'carbon lock-in' since it creates persistent market and policy failures that inhibit the diffusion of carbon-saving technologies despite their apparent environmental and economic advantages. Unruh (2000) argues further that the "lock-in occurs through combined interactions among technological systems and governing institutions, which perpetuate fossil fuel-based infrastructure in spite of their known environmental externalities and the apparent existence of cost-neutral, or even cost-efficient, remedies". These technological systems have to be seen as large complex systems of technologies embedded in powerful conditioning social context of public and private institutions. To avoid confusion with other definitions of technological systems (Hughes, 1983) we label these systems as Technology Specific Innovation Systems (TSIS), which are defined as:

> *"...a dynamic network of agents interacting in a specific economic/industrial area under a particular institutional infrastructure and involved in the generation, diffusion and utilisation of technology" (Carlsson & Stanckiewicz, 1991).*

Once such a system is locked-in it is very difficult to displace it and alternative technologies can be locked-out for a long time even if they demonstrate improvements upon the established systems (Unruh, 2000). It is impossible to isolate a single factor, which could un-lock the system, but one possibility could be that the existing system loses viability because the selection environment is changing and provides new types of challenge which cannot be met with the dominant technology or require advances which are only possible at too much marginal cost (Schot et al., 1994). When alternative technologies do meet the new challenges a building process starts of a new Technology Specific Innovation System that is created

[13] Based on Abbott, etc.

around the new technology. In Jacobsson (2000) the rise of renewable energy technologies are explained by analysing the development of a new Technology Specific Innovation System that co-evolves with the development of new technology.

The growth of an emerging Technology Specific Innovation System can be stylised by identifying different development phases, such as a formative phase and a diffusion phase (Utterback, 1994a; Utterback, 1994b). The formative phase is characterised by a range of competing designs, small markets, many entrants and high uncertainty in terms of technologies, markets and regulations (Kemp et al., 1998). This phase involves the exploration of niche markets where the technology can develop and be tested by users and demonstrate to be superior in some dimension(s), such as environmentally or economically (Jacobsson & Johnson, 2002). The development phase is characterised by a fast growing market, a selection of a dominant design and a fast reduction in production costs. To unlock the existing energy system, it is important that several Technology Specific Innovation Systems develop successfully and take over part of the existing energy system. The main question is: what are the determining factors that explain this successful growth?

Edquist (Edquist, 2001) states that these determining factors can be traced by identifying all those activities that take place in innovation systems that influence the development, diffusion and use of an innovation. These activities are also called 'Functions of Innovation Systems',

The concept of "System Functions" is developed by Jacobsson and Johnson (2000) who define it as "a contribution of a component or a set of components to a system's performance. They argue that a Technology Specific Innovation System, "may be described and analysed in terms of its 'functional pattern', i.e. in how these functions have been served" (Jacobsson & Johnson, 2000). The functions are related to the character of, and the interaction between, the components of an innovation system, i.e. actors (e.g. firms and other organisations), networks and institutions, which may be specific to one innovation system or 'shared' between a number of different systems (Jacobsson & Johnson, 2000; Edquist, 2001). By assessing the 'functionality', i.e. how well these functions are served, the performance of an innovation system could be assessed (Jacobsson & Johnson, 2000). Here, the performance of SI is defined as the rate of development, diffusion and implementation of a new technology. To understand how a technology is developed, diffused and implemented, the functional pattern of the technological innovation system around the technology will be described and analysed through time; The more functions are served, the better the performance of the innovation system, since the overall function of the innovation system is to produce, diffuse and use innovations (Edquist, 2001)[14]. In the following paragraph the system functions and how they have been measured will be described.

2.1 Functions of the SI

Function 1. Entrepreneurial Activities

The role of the entrepreneur is to turn the potential of new knowledge development, networks and markets into concrete actions to generate and take advantage of business opportunities. Entrepreneurs can be new entrants that have the vision of such opportunities in new markets or incumbent companies who diversify their business strategy to take advantage of new developments. Experimenting by entrepreneurs is necessary to cope with the large uncertainties that follow from new combinations of technological knowledge, new

[14] see Chapter 3 Methodology for a more detailed description on how the functional pattern is described and how our manner differs from previous studies.

applications and markets. This uncertainty is a fundamental feature of technological and industrial development.

Function 2. Knowledge Development (learning)

Mechanisms of learning are at the heart of any innovation process. For instance, according to Lundvall (1992) 'the most fundamental resource in the modern economy is knowledge and, accordingly, the most important process is learning'. This function includes 'Learning by Searching' and 'Learning by Doing'.

Function 3. Knowledge Diffusion through Networks

The network makes out the structure of the IS; it can be considered as an intermediate form of organisation between organisations and markets. According to Carlsson and Stankiewicz (1991) its essential characteristic is the exchange of information. This is important in a strict R&D setting, but especially in a heterogeneous context where R&D meets government, competitors and market.

Function 4. Guidance of the Search

Since resources are limited in nature, it is important that when various different technological options exist, specific foci are chosen for further investments. Without this selection there will be insufficient resources left over for the individual options. The function can be fulfilled by a variety of system components such as the industry, the government and/or the market. As a function, guidance of the search refers to those activities within the innovation system that can positively affect the visibility and clarity of specific wants among technology users. An example is the announcement of the government goal to aim for a certain percentage of renewable energy in a future year. This event grants a certain degree of legitimacy to the development of sustainable energy technologies and stimulates the allocation of resources for this development. An important, though elusive, class of phenomena here concerns expectations (cp. van Lente, 1998, 2000). Often actors are 'initially' driven by little more than a hunch. Vague ideas are often tried out and their success (and failure) can be communicated to other actors, thereby reducing the (perceived) degree of uncertainty. Occasionally, under the influence of 'success stories', expectations on a specific topic converge and generate a momentum for change in a specific direction.

Function 5. Market Formation

New technology often has difficulty to compete with embedded technologies. Therefore, it is important to create protected spaces for new technologies. One possibility is the formation of temporary niche markets (Schot, 1994) for specific applications of the technology (Schot et al., 1994). Another possibility is to create a temporary competitive advantage by favourable tax regimes or minimal consumption quotes.

Function 6. Resources Mobilisation

Resources, both financial and human capital, are necessary as a basic input to all the activities within the innovation system. For biomass digestion, the allocation of sufficient physical resources is also necessary to make further developments possible.

Function 7: Support from Advocacy Coalitions

In order to develop well, a new technology has to become part of an incumbent regime, or has to even overthrow it. Parties with vested interests will often oppose this force of 'creative destruction'. In that case, advocacy coalitions can function as a catalyst; they put a new technology on the agenda, lobby for resources, favourable tax regimes and by doing so create legitimacy for a new 'technological trajectory' (Sabatier, 1988; Sabatier & Jenkinssmith, 1988; Sabatier, 1998). If successful, advocacy coalitions grow in size and influence and may become powerful enough to brisk up the spirit of creative destruction.

2.2 Dynamics through interaction

The individual fulfilment of each function is an important determinant for the dynamics of the system, however another important explanatory factor is the positive or negative interaction between the functions. Positive interactions between the functions could lead to a self-reinforcing dynamic within the SI, whereas negative interactions can cause the SI to collapse. For example, an increase in knowledge and positive research results can lead to high expectations for the emergent technology, attracting new actors to join, resulting that more resources (financial, human and physical) are available for the development of the emergent technology. This again leads to more knowledge creation and research. Another possibility of positive interaction could occur when high expectations trigger the rise of lobbies and coalition parties for this particular technology, resulting in the creation of a market. This formation of market stimulates again entrepreneurs to expand their project from laboratory scale to a commercial scale. These positive interactions between functions are called *virtuous cycle.*

Several possibilities of these self-reinforcing cycles are represented in the Figure 1 below but many other forms are possible as well.

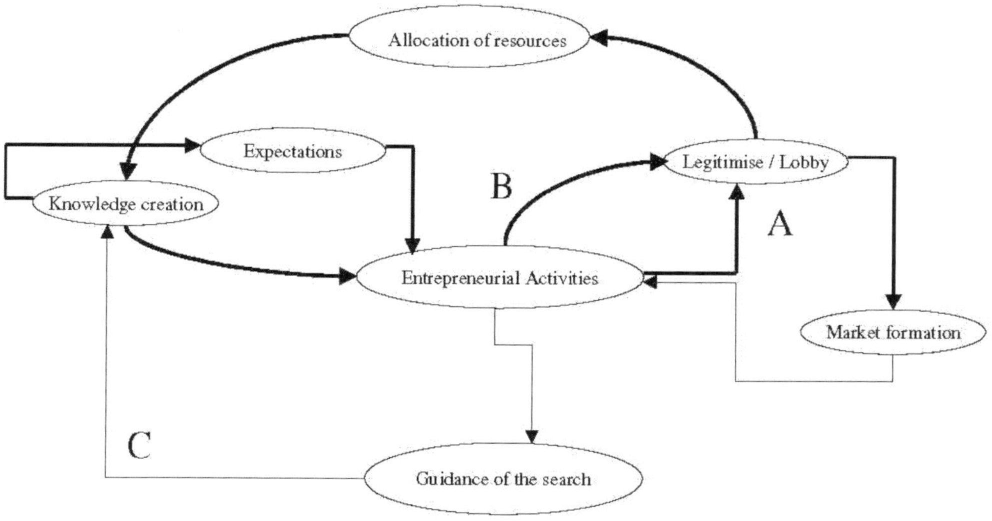

Figure 1: Overview of possible self-reinforcing cycles within a SI

We call these self-reinforcing cycles 'motors' of the SI and they can be considered as the driving forces of the system dynamics; the system functions are the building blocks of these motors.

Besides the self-reinforcing cycles also vicious circles can take place. In this case a negative fulfilment of a function leads to negative feedbacks to other functions, resulting in a decreasing functional pattern. In this case the motor stops. An example could be the cut back of national subsidy programmes (decrease resources), reducing also the expectations about the success of the emerging technology, which again results that entrepreneurs stop their activities as well, so that the expectations decrease even more and that finally also the remaining subsidy will be removed.

The policy relevance of this framework is that policy initiatives directed at stimulating sustainable change of the energy system should focus on stimulating system weak system functions to increase the chance on self-reinforcing feedbacks and thereby positive system dynamics.

3 Methodology

In recent empirical work concerning functions of innovation systems, generally qualitative analysis is used. This method strongly rests on the results from interviews. The set of functions serves mainly as a way to structure empirical material, see (Andersson & Jacobsson, 2000; Jacobsson & Bergek, 2004). The down side of this method is that it is not possible to construct patterns of function activities, which limits the potential of explaining system functioning. We propose to use as much quantitative indicators as possible in order to be able to map functional patterns over time. For this purpose we developed a method inspired on the idea of a 'Historical Event Analysis' as deployed by Van de Ven and colleagues (van de Ven et al., 1999; Poole et al., 2000). Stemming from organisational theory, their usual focus is on the firm and firm networks; in our case the analysis is deployed at system level. Basically the approach consists of retrieving as many historical events related to a technological development as possible based on professional journals, newspapers and websites. The events are stored in a database, classified and systematically allocated to Functions of Innovation Systems. Functional patterns can then be extracted from the database. The methodology results in a coherent sequence of events and trends that describe how things change over time. In our case the event sequence analysis is used to analyse the development, diffusion and implementation of biomass digestion in the Netherlands from 1974-2004.

Functions are measured by counting instances of event types in time. However a distinction should be made. Functions can be measured as negatives as well as positives. Some events have a negative contribution to the development of the technology, for instance an expression of disappointment, or the opposition of an important political group, i.e resulting in a *vicious cycle*. These events are counted separately and are represented as negative scores. In this way an overview of supporting and impeding activities is provided.

3.1 Boundaries of this study

This paper presents a chronological description of the events that have taken place in biomass digestion development from 1974-2004. Some exceptional events that have happened in 2004 are also included to keep the description as up to date as possible. However, 2004 is not analysed as thoroughly as the other years.

The analysis on biomass digestion is restricted to only digestion of manure, organic- and agricultural waste. Digestion of wastewater is not included. The reason for not including these streams is the fact that it involves a totally different innovation system with different actors and different institutions. Furthermore the technological factors affecting the diffusion are not the same due to the difference in feedstock.

3.2 Technical aspects of biomass digestion technology

This paragraph will give an overview of the technical aspects of biomass digestion.

Anaerobic digestion is a low-temperature biochemical process, through which a combustible gas - biogas - can be produced from biomass feedstock. The biogas is a mixture of carbon dioxide (CO_2) and methane (CH_4), which can be used to generate heat and/or electricity via secondary conversion technologies like gas engines and turbines. High moisture biomass feedstocks are especially well suited for the anaerobic digestion process (IEA; TheBiomassSite; BioGen 2002).

The feedstock is placed into a digester, a warmed, sealed airless container. The digestion tank is continuously stirred and heated to around 35°C to create the ideal condition for biogas conversion. Although there is a constant inflow and outflow of material, the average retention time is 18 days. This allows a significant percentage of the organic solids to be converted to biogas. The outflows of the digesters can be in two forms: biogas and a liquor/fibre mixture, known as 'digestate'. The gas from the digesters is stored to control the flow into the engine and this engine is used to generate heat and electricity for on-site or off-site use (see Figure 2 – Diagram of digestion process) (IEA; TheBiomassSite; BioGen 2002).

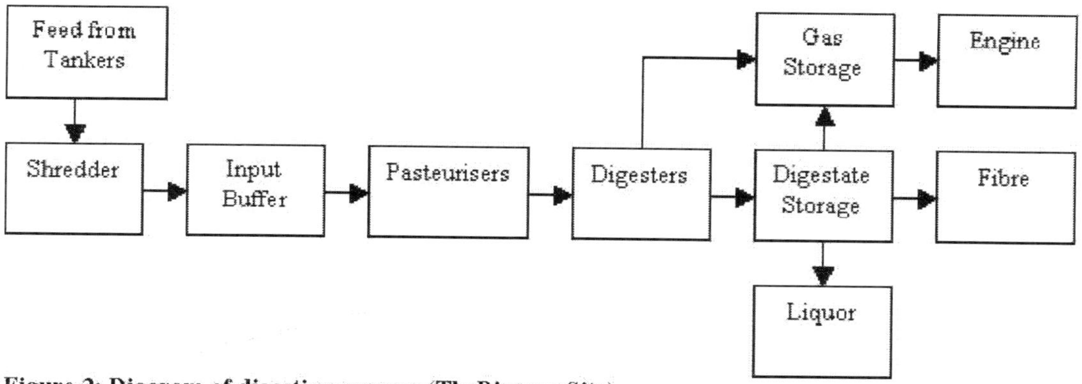

Figure 2: Diagram of digestion process (TheBiomassSite)

4 Event Description: The Case of biomass digestion

This chapter presents a chronological description of the events that took place in the biomass digestion trajectory. The description will be subdivided into different year periods, where the end of such a period is chosen on the basis of change in activities or key events, therefore a difference in the amount of years per period will occur.

4.1 The pioneers' era, 1974-1987

The period 1974-1980 is characterised by pioneers setting up the first experiments on manure digestion. Since the oil crises and an increasing manure surplus problem, digestion of manure seems a promising option to reduce energy costs on farms and the excess of manure. Several farmers are enthusiastic about this option and digestion installations are set up on several farms (Verbong et al., 2001). Developers of digestion equipment, such as Paques, see a great market opportunity to install digestion equipment on farms. This results that between 1979 and 1983 the number of digestion plants on farms increases to about 25, so that the application of digestion moves from laboratory scale to practical scale (Nes, 1988). However, a survey on the digestion plants built on farms shows that there are still a lot of technical and economical problems. Nonetheless, it is believed that the problems are solvable and so the

'Netherlands Ministry of Housing, Spatial Planning and the Environment' (Ministry of VROM) constructs a trial plant in Assendelft within the framework of the "National Research Programme for Recycling of Waste" (NOH programme) (Nes, 1988). However, shortly after the plant is shut down, due to the decrease of conventional energy prices, lack of profits, technical problems and complicated permit regulations (Nes, 1988; Verbong et al., 2001). An additional barrier to the technical and economic problems is the inconsistency of governmental policies (E&S, 1982). The government shows a lack of vision and strategy for the development and introduction of renewable energies, be it on short- or long-term, small- or large-scale, centralised or decentralised energy projects (E&S, 1982). There is no clear attitude towards the energy intensive industry and a high budget for the further development of nuclear energy is provided (E&S, 1982). Due to this lack of commitment and uncertainties, further projects and constructions of digestion plants are delayed and current plants are shut down (E&S, 1983). This results from that manure digestion is not seen as a renewable energy technology that will contribute to the national energy supply, but that it is a solution to the reduction of the manure surplus with the added value for farmers to produce their own energy (Blok 1985, DE 3, p.4; Verbong 2001). The interest in manure digestion decreases due to the unsolved technical problems, the decrease of energy prices and the lack of effort and support by the government (Nes, 1988). Additionally Minister Braks of Agriculture announces in 1986 that no more investment and support will be given to further development of manure digestion or existing projects, due to the technical problems and the reduced fossil fuel energy prices, that make digestion expensive and unprofitable (Nes, 1988). This results that no activities for biomass digestion occur in 1987.

In this period, functions such as entrepreneurial activities, knowledge creation and market formation are fulfilled positively, since entrepreneurs set up small-scale digestion installations on farms, farmers are interested in this technology and engine builders see a market opportunity. However, other functions were not fulfilled at all, so that no built up of activities that would reinforce each other, took place. Instead, a vicious cycle occurs where none of the functions are fulfilled positively, due to the unsolved technical problems and high costs, resulting in reduced expectations and enthusiasm, causing the shut down of current projects and plants and stop of support by the government. In the case where the government announces that no further support will be given to biomass digestion, functions such as guidance of the search, advocacy coalition and resource allocation are fulfilled negatively, since they do not contribute to the development of biomass digestion.

4.2 Impulses and inconsistency around digestion, 1988-1995

In 1988 activities are picked up again and an assessment study about the existing manure digestion plants and the future feasibility of biomass digestion is carried out by the environmental consultancy CE within the NOH programme (Nes, 1988). The outcome of the study is a handbook about manure digestion. Current predictions are that the livestock will decrease but that separation and collection of organic waste will increase, which can also be used for digestion and will therefore provide enough feedstock for digestion (Nes, 1988). Following this prediction, the 'National Coordination Commission for Waste Policy' (LCCA) sets up a 'National Sales Office' (LVK) for organic waste and compost to avoid competition between producers of digestion and fermentation and to obtain product certificates for organic waste (Haskoning, 1991). Nonetheless this preventive effort it is seen later in 1996 that several projects fail to start up, since the composting sector is in control of all waste streams (Janse, 1996a; Janse, 1996b; Abbas, 1998).

In 1989 large-scale collection and separation of organic waste is introduced in the Netherlands, where it is expected that digestion will be an interesting option to process waste and to produce energy (Brinkmann, 2000). This results that several plants are set up. One is a manure digestion plant together with a wind turbine in Deersum, Friesland, which provides the village with electricity. The digestion plant shows to be efficient and profitable due to the collective manure digestion and large-scale application (Nes, 1989). In addition, researchers at the University of Wageningen and engineering consultant Heidemij, set up a plant using the Biocel conversion system and another two plants are set up in Lelystad and Tilburg (Haskoning, 1991); (Milieutechnologie, 1991); (E&MT, 1991). These latter two plants are supported by the Ministry of VROM to make digestion the spearhead within the programme 'CO_2-emission reduction via waste regulation' of Senter[15] (Brinkmann, 2000). Another plant is built in 1993 called 'Greenery' in Breda, where the leftovers of the fruit and vegetable auction are digested (Zoeten et al., 1992). Additionally, the Ministry of EZ, VROM and NOVEM commission a programme called 'Energy production from waste and biomass' (EWAB) with the aim to promote the application of waste and biomass as energy source. Within the framework of the EWAB and NOH programme several research, evaluation, feasibility and comparison studies of the plants mentioned above are carried out and platforms are set up for biomass digestion (Haskoning, 1992b; Haskoning, 1992c); (NOVEM, 1992; Haskoning, 1993; E&MSpectrum, 1993).

In October 1994 the Ministry of EZ announces a cut back of 81 million euro from R&D demonstration and application budget for new energy technologies (Vos, 1994). Compensation for this cut back will be the exemption for renewable energies from small-scale consumer levy introduced in 1996. Nonetheless the cut of the budget forms a real threat to the research, development and market introduction of renewable energies, since they are not profitable without subsidies yet (E&MSpectrum, 1994). The EWAB programme budget is reduced from 3.6 million euro to 2.5 million euros (E&MSpectrum, 1994). Research institutes such as the Energy Research Centre of the Netherlands (ECN) and Netherlands Organisation for Applied Scientific Research (TNO) suffer most from the R&D cut backs. The fear is that since no further policies are formulated, the objectives will be erased, since there will be no further development and no markets, so that the government will reduce the budget even more (DE, 1994). In addition, the Ministry of Economic Affairs announces that only combustion and gasification are supported but not digestion (E&MSpectrum, 1994). This cut of budget could be an attempt by the government to change from R&D instruments to market instruments, however the consequences are seen shortly after when the combined digestion plant and wind turbine in Deersum, Friesland is shut down in 1994, due to technical problems and the political unwillingness to further support digestion (DE, 1994). Additionally, biomass digestion is not seen as a promising technology for large-scale energy supply, since there are no strong policies in the Netherlands, which force farmers to store manure and use it for manure digestion, instead of spreading it on the land (Daey Ouwens, 1993). Finally, biogas production is predicted to be only profitable if there are more subsidies allocated to digestion, the fossil fuel prices are high and that collective digestion and co-digestion of energy rich organic waste are allowed (E&MSpectrum, 1993).

Between 1989 and 1994 a beginning of a positive built up of several functions occurs. Due to the collection of organic waste, digestion is rediscovered as promising technology, where research leads to positive results (Knowledge creation), triggering the construction of several plants (Entrepreneurial activities), and that the Government sets up two national programme (Guidance of the Search). This again initiates further research within these programmes. During these 5 years some activities trigger other activities to occur, so that several functions

[15] Senter is a financing agency under the Dutch Ministry of Economic Affairs

are fulfilled triggering other functions. However, due to one destructive activity by the Government of cutting back subsidies, the previously originated positive built-up collapses and hardly any activities are fulfilled afterwards.

4.3 An attempt of revival, 1995-2004

This period is marked by the closure of several plants set up in previous years, since biomass is getting scarce, expensive and no end-use is found for the 'digestate' produced during digestion, i.e Breda and Tilburg (Janse, 1998). Furthermore, a general political uncertainty overshadows this period, since the government formulates no common and consistent regulations. For instance, the Ministry of Economic Affairs publishes the 'Third White Paper on Energy'[16] (Derde Energie Nota) but doesn't provide any common strategy on the technical and economical development of bio-energy on how to achieve this goal (EZ, 1995). On the other hand, they do provide very restrictive and complicated regulations for co-digestion and on the quality and composition of non-manure organic based fertiliser (MilieuMagazine, 2001; Reumerman, 2004). From a benchmarking study it is found that the amount of investments and policies in the Netherlands is very broad and the technical potential is still small, resulting in high costs (E&MSpectrum, 1998). This triggers several actors to unify the scattered initiatives of pioneers by setting up platforms and information centres and to build a coalition to counter the critical voices that do not see biomass digestion as a promising technology (NOVEM, 1998). Furthermore by 'gathering the forces' they hope to facilitate the regulation making and achieve an exemption of biomass conversion processes from the 'regulating energy tax' (REB) (DE, 2000).

In 1999 the construction of the largest digestion plant for organic waste in Groningen with a VAGRON conversion system starts. The plant is a demonstration plant for separation of integral household waste into different fractions, where the organic wet fraction (ONF) is digested. The biogas produced is converted into electricity and delivered to the grid (Stromen, 1999; DE, 1999; ECN, 1999; Vermaat, 1999). Additionally, two demonstration centres for digestion of manure are set up on farms, since it is found that digestion is profitable for farmers and the climate (ECOFYS, 2003; DE, 2002a; Stromen, 2003).

Nonetheless, the impulses and efforts to establish digestion as a solution for several problems, i.e. manure surplus, waste treatment and climate change, the development and application of digestion is still delayed due to inconsistent policies and regulations. The government has to provide more financial security, facilitate the permit application procedures and provide a level playing field, also on European level (DE, 2002b). Additionally, since the election in 1998 it is not clear which direction the government will take with respect to financial support, such as the energy tax, since such regulations are still very important for the development of digestion to become a self-sustained technology (DE, 2002c). An example is the delayed introduction of the 'Environmental Quality Electricity Production' (MEP) regulation. This regulation subsidises the electricity production of renewable energies, so that the unfeasible economic aspect of most biomass technologies is reduced and provides a ten-year investment security (EZ, 2003). However, with a earning back period of 6-9 years for the construction of a digestion plant, the ten years fixed rates are not ample enough (Reumerman, 2004). The MEP-tariffs should be established three years beforehand otherwise the financing of large biomass projects would be in danger. Therefore the Dutch Office for Renewable Energies (PDE) requests from the Ministry of Economic Affairs to qualify all forms of digestion, except from dump gas and waster water treatment installation for the MEP (DE, 2003b).

[16] The aim is to achieve a 10% share of renewable energies in 2020 where biomass should contribute 44% (EZ, 1995)

Finally after long years of struggling in 2004 the laws for co-digestion will be altered. Minister Van Geel (VROM) and Minister Veerman (LNV) are going to revise the complicated regulations and policies around manure digestion and soon farmers will be allowed to add organic material to the manure for co-digestion. In addition clear directives will be developed for the set up and testing of environmental permits (Stromen, 2004a; Wijland, 2004c). Further, the coming months the Ministries will work on a list of organic substances that are allowed to be co-digested with manure. Due to this 'green list' and simplified permit procedure, experts expect an increase of biogas plants on farms. However, the real breakthrough for dozens of large biogas plants will only be achieved if the government releases the second half of the 'green list', where also products from the food industry, such as frying fat and swill will be included (TW, 2004; Zoethout, 2004c; Stromen, 2004d).

The beginning of this final period is marked again by the incoherent guidance of the government and a lack of entrepreneurial activities, since most of the plants shut down. However, actors realise that the efforts are too scattered and unrelated throughout the Netherlands and that coalitions need to be formed to give more weight to the interests of biomass digestion. These efforts pay off after 20-30 years of struggling that some changes will be made in the regulations and institutions regarding biomass co-digestion. However the final breakthrough will only occur if there is a continuous support and favourable conditions so that more activities can build up as to create a virtuous cycle that will be strong enough to withstand any destructive activities.

5 System functioning analysis

In this chapter the system functioning will be assessed, first by analysing the fulfilment of the individual functions over time and secondly by studying the interactions between the functions and its effect during the time periods and whether a built up of cycles and motors occurred.

5.1 Description of the individual System Function fulfilment

In the Figure of Function Entrepreneurial Activities the amount of projects set up and stopped throughout the period are represented. The upper and lower lines are a cumulative representation of projects and the smaller lines are the actual number of project started and stopped per year. Most of the plants have been built around 1992 but nearly as many have been closed down in that same period. After 2002 a stagnation of construction occurs and the organic waste plant in Tilburg is shut down.

This shows that the fulfilment of the function has been varied, resulting only in a handful of plants, instead of a continuous increase of plants being constructed as to realise a large-scale implementation of biomass digestion.

Most of the activities for Function Knowledge creation occur around 1992, where the most research is done on digestion technology for manure and organic waste. However, after the subsidy cut of the EWAB research programme in 1994, hardly any research is carried out afterwards anymore. Also this function is not fulfilled in a consistent way, however a slight increase of activities seems to start around 2004.

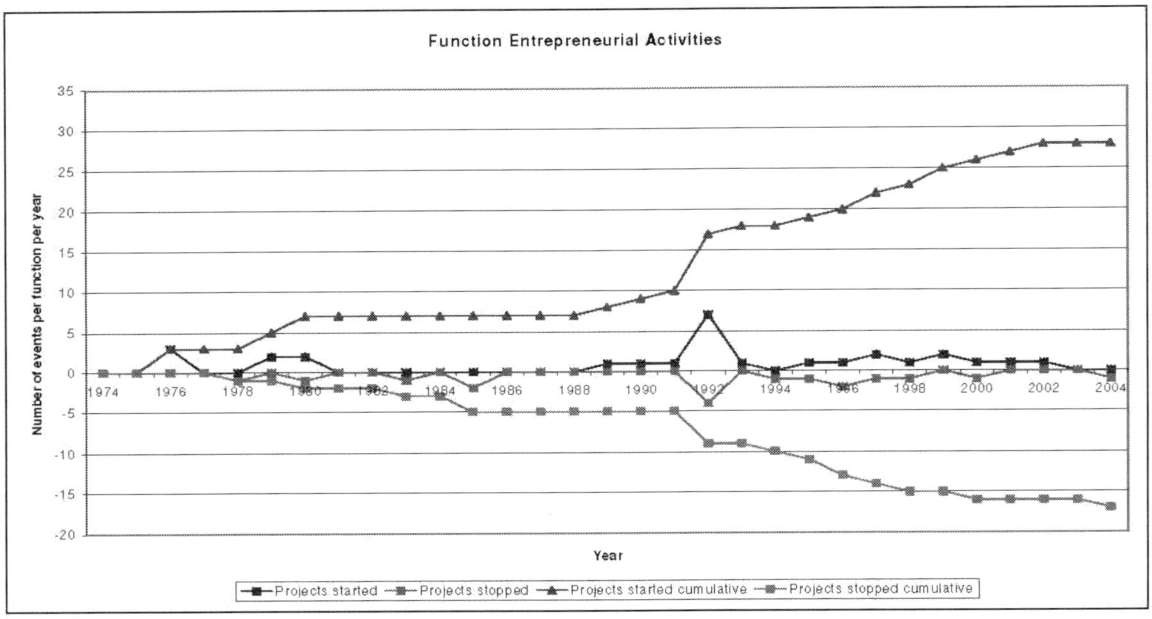

Figure 3: Overview of the fulfilment of Function Entrepreneurial activities

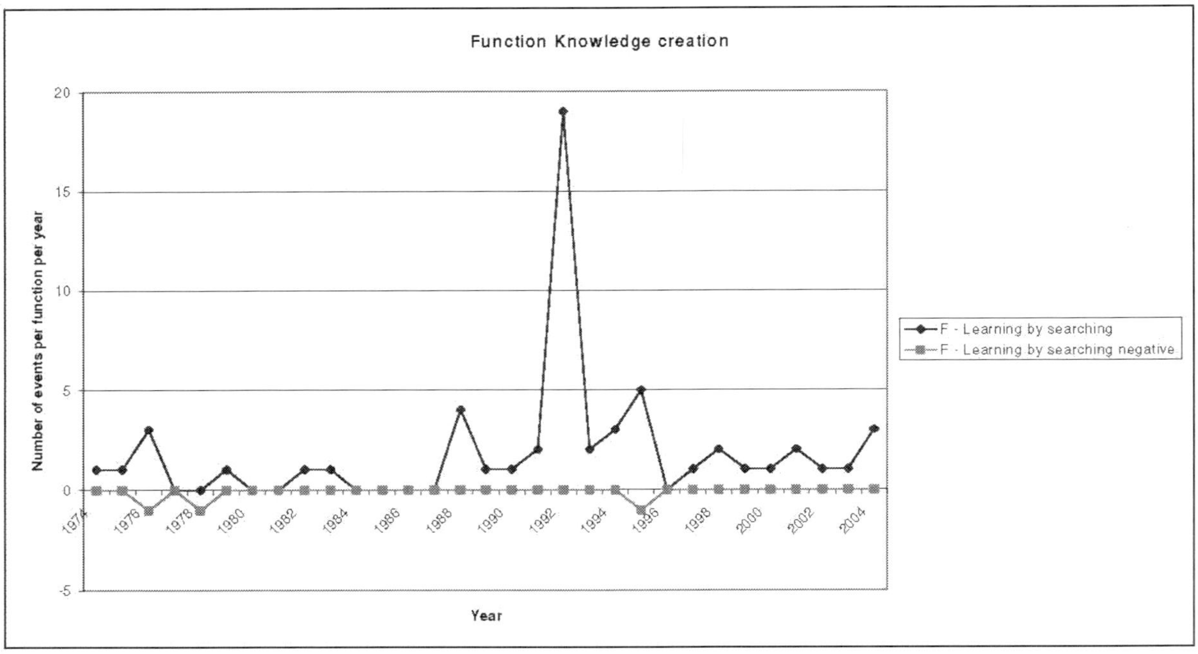

Figure 4: Functions Knowledge Creation – Learning by searching

For the Function Knowledge Diffusion the most activities occur in 1992 and in 2002, where the dispersed pattern results from the scattered research initiatives across the Netherlands, resulting in little knowledge diffusion. Since there were several destructive actions and technical problems throughout the period that made most of the activities collapse, actors were 'chased' back to their research labs to try to solve the problems, but on a dispersed and individual basis. Only after a few years when promising results were obtained would people exchange knowledge again on workshop, conferences etc, until another destructive 'blow' would diffuse everybody again. Also this function has been fulfilled in a sporadic way, where no continuous increase of activities for this function occurs.

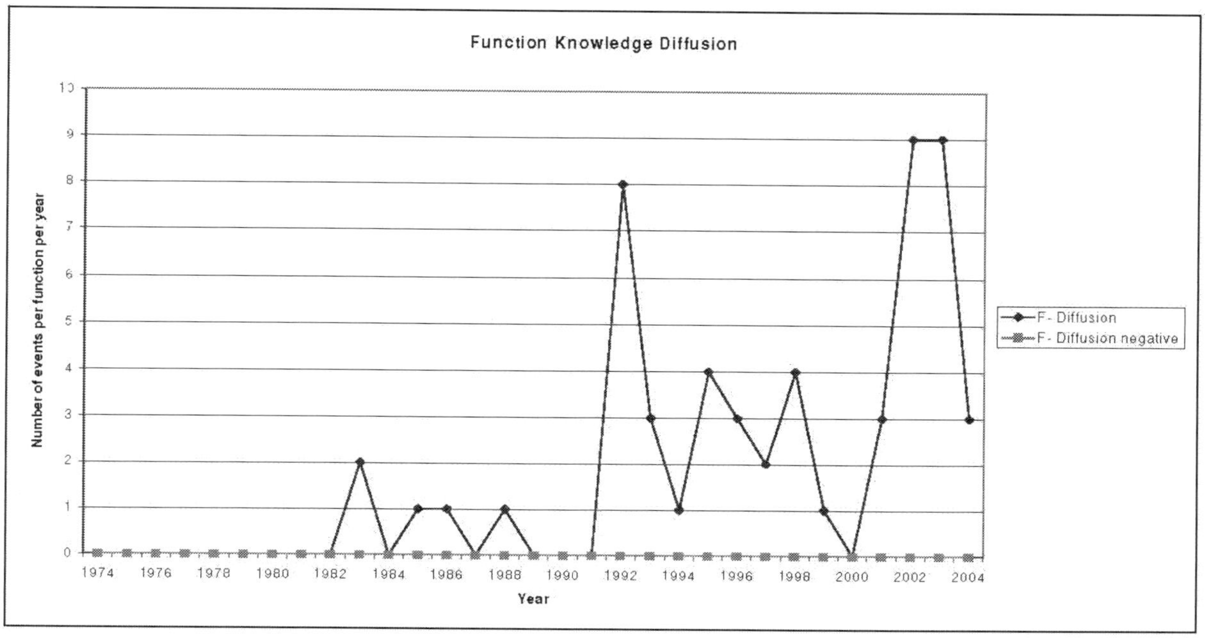

Figure 5: Function Knowledge Diffusion

Throughout the years the government provided two different and contradictory sorts of regulations. One type were mostly general regulations for renewable energies without specification for a particular technology, so that entrepreneurs and investors had to find out themselves whether their technology or project was eligible for that tax exemption, subsidy, or fell under a certain policy or within the goals of a White Paper. This led to confusion and ignorance among entrepreneurs, resulting that in one year several projects were started because the conditions seem preferable, whereas the following year the projects were stopped again because there was no more political support. On the other hand, specific regulations were also formulated but mainly only to stop any activities around biomass digestion, such as announcements, that research budgets or subsidies were reduced or that biomass digestion was not supported anymore and not seen as a promising technology and that other technologies, such as combustion, gasification and fermentation were preferred rather than biomass digestion. For this function as well there were not enough and constant activities that resulted in a positive and strong fulfilment of the function. However, in 2004 a significant increase of activities occurs, due to the change in co-digestion regulations. However, since this change starts in 2004 it is not known how the line will continue in the following years, since the analysis stops in 2004.

Throughout the years hardly any niche markets have been created, resulting that the Function Market formation has hardly been fulfilled. One niche market opportunity was to set up small-scale digestion plants on farms, however due to unfavourable regulations and technical problems, many of those projects were stopped. Furthermore, in comparison other technologies, such as fermentation, gasification and combustion enjoyed more support to create their own niche market, resulting in negative market creation for digestion since it was not supported. Again an increase of activities results in 2004 due to the agreement that co-digestion on farms will be allowed partly for some substances.

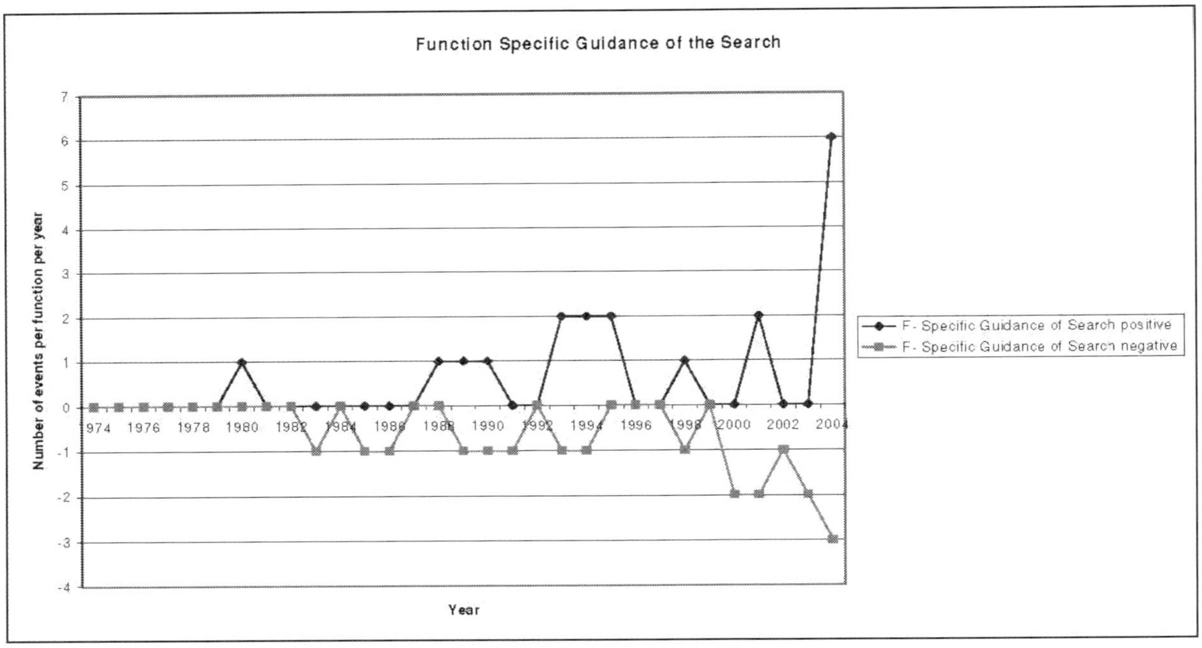

Figure 6: Overview of the fulfilment of the Function Specific Guidance of the Search

For the Function Resource mobilisation even less activities are observed, due to the lack of subsidies, i.e. cut back of research subsidies and a general lack of investments. Additionally a lack of biomass streams reigned throughout the period, due to the competition with fermentation for organic waste and a change of regulations where forestry and agricultural waste are left on the land and no longer collected. Also for this function there can hardly be said that the function has been fulfilled.

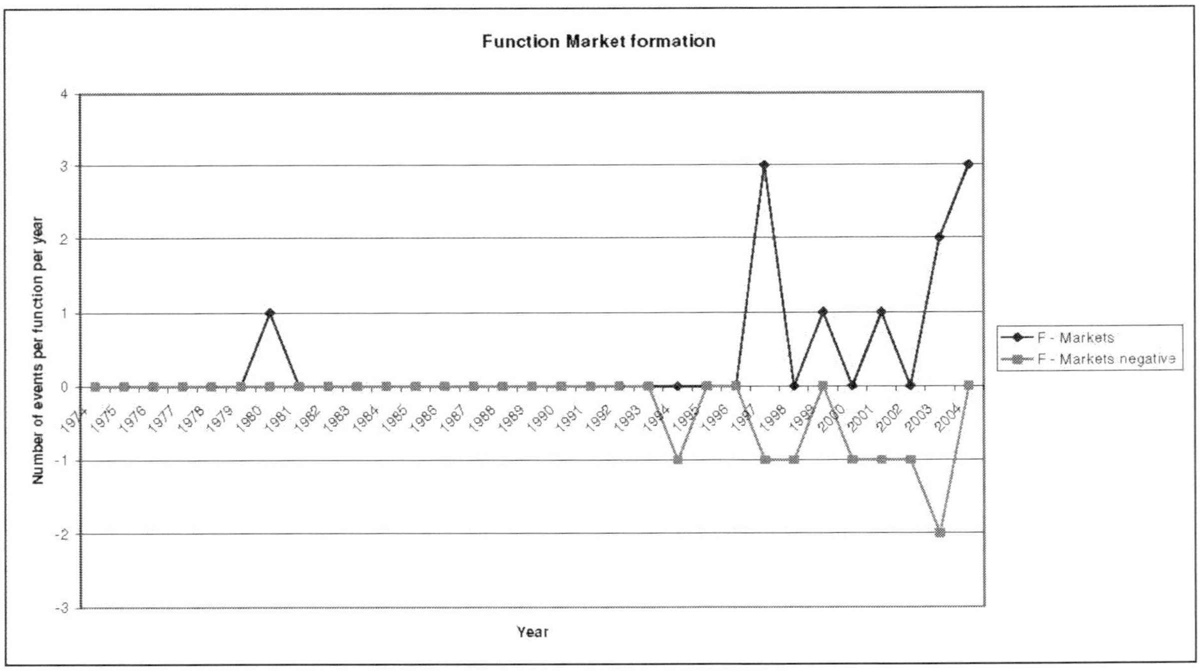

Figure 7: Function Market formation

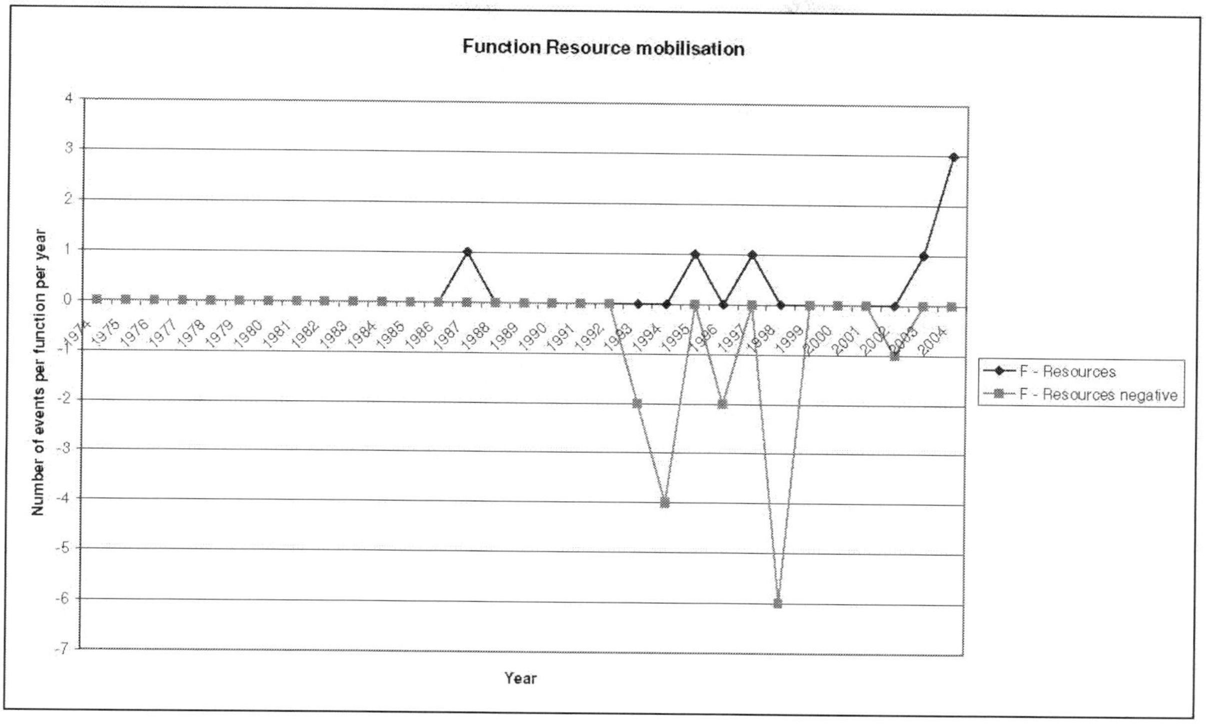

Figure 8: Function Resource Mobilisation

For the Function Advocacy Coalition a dispersed pattern is observed: there were enough advocates that supported the technology throughout the years, however, they hardly formed any coalitions to counteract the destructive actions. On contrary it seems that after each destructive 'blow' the advocates were driven apart and only after a while started to form coalitions again. The coalitions are important to lobby for an equal playing field and favourable regulations for biomass digestion and to overcome the opponents who in this case had enough influence to counteract the development of biomass digestion throughout the whole period (see negative line of the graph). Also for this function it can hardly be talked about fulfilment due to the small number of activities realised for this function. However, in 2004 a steep increase of activities is seen, since coalitions are formed to realise the changes of regulations for co-digestion.

To summarise it can be said that there was a strong fluctuation in the amount, regularity and consistency of activities throughout the years, resulting in an irregular and inconsistent fulfilment and for some functions even none. We would expect a built up of activities, with a similar pattern as the cumulative line of the entrepreneurial activities, however as absolute numbers for each function throughout the whole period, but for none of the functions such a pattern was observed. Around 2004 some functions saw a substantial increase of activities due to the commitment by some Ministries to alter the regulations for co-digestion, but since this case study stops in 2004, the further development and consequences are not known. Finally, during some years a beginning of activities building up was observed, which will be examined in the next section.

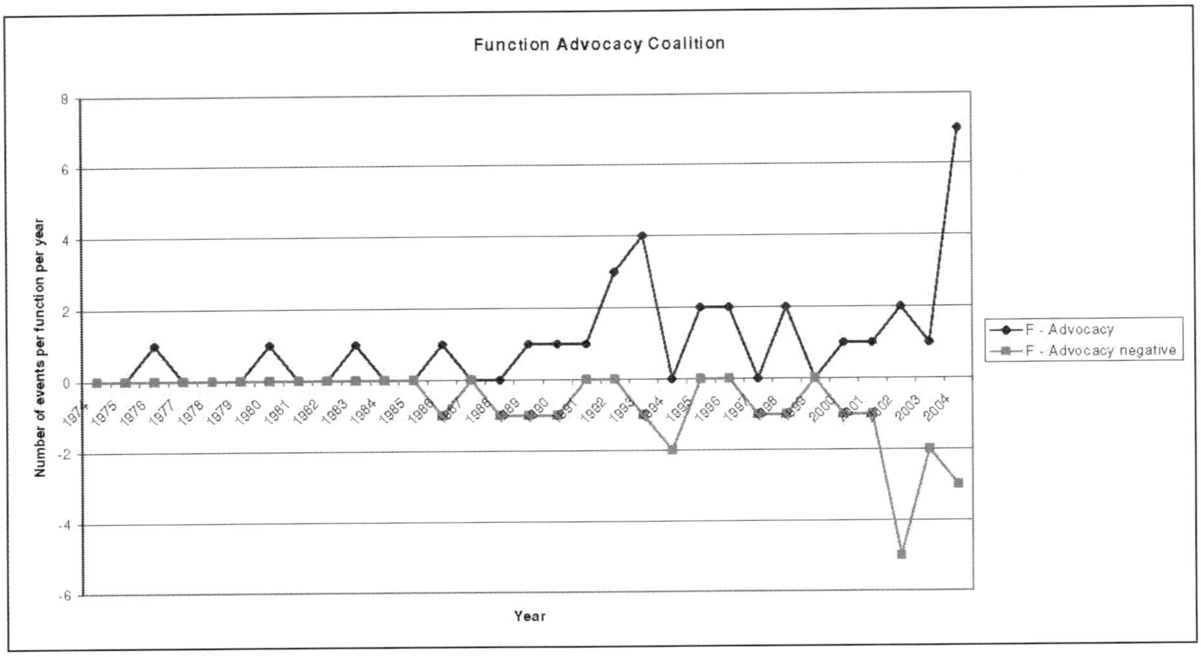

Figure 9: Overview of the fulfilment of Function Advocacy coalition

5.2 Fulfilment of functions per year period

1974-1987

To summarise these first ten years of activities, the frail beginning of a virtuous cycle and the take over of a vicious cycle are observed. The virtuous cycle consists of activities such as Function Knowledge Creation, where research is done on manure digestion, which provides positive results so that expectations grow. This results in that Government sets up a national research programme about waste recycling (NOH), supporting manure and biomass digestion as an option to reduce the waste surplus, i.e. Function Guidance. At this moment entrepreneurs set up digestion plants, propelling the technology from laboratory scale to practical scale, Function Entrepreneurial Activities (see Figure 10, Loop C bold writing). This shows that a built-up of activities takes place for about 7 years, where some activities trigger other activities to take place. However, in 1981 when the technology needs to prove itself, there are still technical problems and the results are less positive than expected. This results that shortly after the expectations decrease, the government does not provide any more guidance, starting a vicious cycle where hardly anymore activities occur and none of the functions are fulfilled, causing a collapse of the virtuous cycle.

1988-1994

Nonetheless the collapse of the virtuous cycle in the previous period, a year later a lot of activities are picked up again. Some actors continue with knowledge creation, providing promising results that increase the expectations, interest and support of several actors. This triggers entrepreneurs to set up projects (one Biocel plant and one in Tilburg), resulting that government sets up several programmes and White Papers, so that digestion receives an impulse and more research is carried out; again loop C in Figure 10 starts to evolve during those 6 years. However, in 1994 the budget of the national research programme EWAB is cut down by the government, resulting in an immediate collapse of all activities.

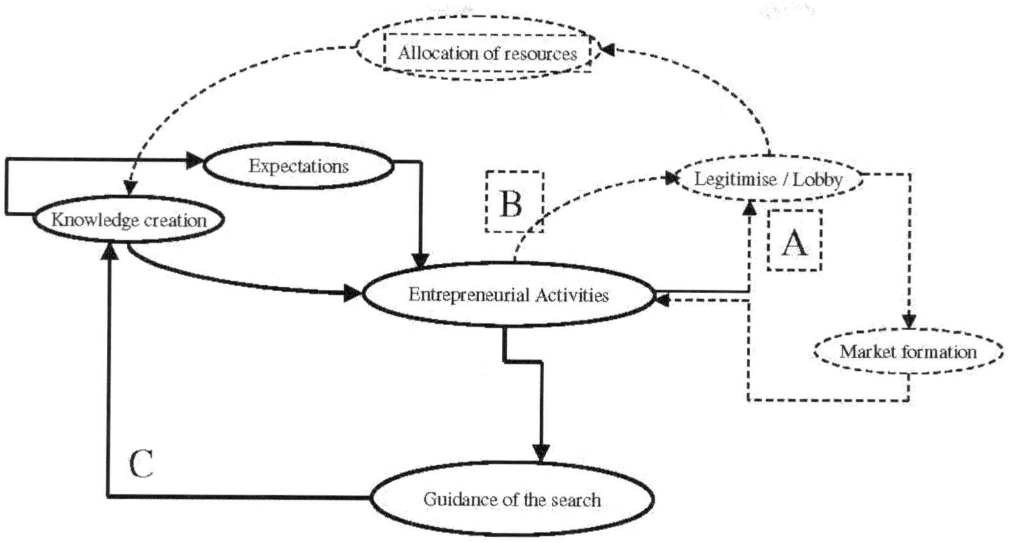

Figure 10: Overview of virtuous cycles, where Loop C is highlighted

1995-1998

In this period the vicious cycle persists, hardly any coherent activities occur, most of the plants built in the previous years are closed down by now and the government lacks to provide any support or guidance, nonetheless the publication of the Third White Paper on Energy. Furthermore, complicated, contradictory and confusing regulations for biomass digestion and co-digestion are maintained.

1999-2003

Nevertheless, that this period is overshadowed by the uncertainty about which direction the government will take after the elections (lack of guidance of search), some pioneers and advocates gather their forces and continue lobbying for biomass digestion (Advocacy coalition), resulting that in 1999 the largest organic waste plant is constructed in Groningen and a few test plants on farms are installed (Entrepreneurial Activities). It seems that activities are picked up again, resulting that in 2004 an agreement was reached by the respective Ministries to release a list of organic materials that are allowed to be co-digested with manure and to simplify the regulations around co-digestion (Guidance of Search). This results that most of the functions, i.e. Knowledge creation, Market creation, Resource mobilisation, Advocacy coalition and Guidance of the Search, experience an increase of activities in 2004. However, whether this will lead to a virtuous cycle is unfortunately beyond the reach of this study due to time limits.

5.3 Analysis of built-up of cycles/motors

To summarise the previous analyses, the amount and frequency of activities per function are small and irregular; a constant built-up of activities is missing. This results that the fulfilment of the functions is fluctuating. Nonetheless, during two periods 1974-1981 and 1989-1994 an increase of several activities occurred that triggered other activities to take place, resulting in a temporary built-up. However, in those two periods the Function Market formation and Resource allocation were not fulfilled. Therefore it was a limited and weak built-up, since not all functions were fulfilled and as soon as a destructive activity occurred, such as lack of support by the government or cut down of research subsidies, the built-up of activities collapsed and no more activities occurred. This results that the two built-ups were not strong enough to withstand such destructive actions.

However, not only the function fulfilment is important; also the technology characteristics play an important role. During technology tryouts the results should be promising enough to make people enthusiastic about the new technology and pursue their efforts to optimise the technology. In the case of biomass digestion for waste treatment there were high expectations with respect to the added value of producing biogas compared to aerobic fermentation where the gases just evaporate. However when these advantages had to be proven in practice, digestion failed, resulting that aerobic fermentation was preferred, being a proven technology and cheaper. In the case of using manure digestion, the expectations were that farmers could produce their own energy and that the manure surplus could be reduced, but again digestion failed to prove these advantages, due to technical problems and that the 'digestate' produced was seen as an additional problem to the already existing manure surplus problem.

The event analysis of the past thirty years leads to think that the technology was not working well enough to be accepted by the system, resulting that system functions were not fulfilled sufficiently and no motors were built. Instead of arguing that the Dutch innovation system did not function well enough to make digestion successful, one could also argue that the Dutch innovation system excelled in screening the benefits of the new technology and was able to filter out a technology too weak to replace the incumbent technology. Based on this it could be said that the system rejected digestion technology. However, when the diffusion of digestion technology in the Netherlands is compared to that in other countries like Germany and Denmark it becomes clear that in those countries digestion has become quite successful. The question why and how digestion has become successful in these countries is a topic for further research.

In the nearby future an additional case on biomass digestion in *Germany* will be carried out for comparison with the Dutch biomass digestion case, where the same methodology of history event analysis and the concept of System Functions of the innovation system will be applied, to identify the differences in underlying factors that enabled a more successful implementation in Germany than in The Netherlands and what could be learned from it for future policy making.

6 Conclusion

Biomass digestion has struggled for decades and is still struggling to become a proven, large-scale, commercial technology that not only converts manure and biomass waste into biogas, but also contributes to the national energy supply and the reduction of climate change. The event analysis showed that the amount of activities was not sufficient enough to trigger virtuous cycles and built-up of motors to propel the system forward into the diffusion phase.

However, the failure cannot be blamed only on the malfunctioning of the innovation system but also to the weak performance of digestion technology, that failed to prove itself at the most crucial moments. This shows that there is a strong interaction between the technology and the innovation system. Therefore, the failure of biomass digestion in The Netherlands results from a combination of non-optimal technology characteristics and a poor functioning innovation system.

Finally, what we learn from this case study is that a substantial amount of activities is required for *all* functions to be fulfilled and that only then the functions will interact with each other to result in virtuous cycles and built-up of motors. Furthermore, policy makers should be aware of the impact that institutions have on a new technology and be aware of the demands of the new technology for certain institutions. What is needed for biomass technologies is a long-term programme with adequate resources and conditions, with enough space for trial and error, with the security that during each government the resources and time span established would be maintained. However a certain flexibility by the policy makers is also required to alter the conditions on short-term when needed, such as to provide protection against competition, e.g. in form of niche markets for the technology to develop.

7 Acknowledgements

The authors are very thankful to Andre Faaij (Utrecht University) for his valuable comments. Furthermore, we are also particularly thankful for the genuine interest, involvement and useful comments by Thijs Oorthuys (Grontmij Nederland bv) and Patrick Reumerman (BTG biomass technology group B.V.) on the empirical part and for the theoretical part by Professor Bo Carlsson (Case Western Reserve University) and Professor Staffan Jacobsson (Chalmers University of Technology). Finally, the paper also benefited from the valuable comments of several other experts from the empirical and theoretical field, who we would like to thank hereby for their time and help.

8 References

Abbas, D. (1998). *Concurrentie of samenwerking?* Duurzame Energie. 8: 10-11.

Andersson, B. A. and S. Jacobsson (2000). *"Monitoring and assessing technology choice: the case of solar cells."* Energy Policy 28(14): 1037-1049.

BioGen (2002). *Anaerobic digestion*, British BioGen Trade Association to the UK Bioenergy Industry.

Brinkmann, A. J. F. (2000). *Vergisting van vast afval: praktijkervaringen en perspectieven in de nederlandse context. Symposium "Biomassa: verbranden, vergassen, vergisten, pyrolyse"* Vereniging van Milieukundigen, Utrecht, 24 mei 2000.

Carlsson, B. and R. Stanckiewicz (1991). *"On the nature, function and composition of technological systems."* Journal of Evolutionary Economics(1): 93-118.

Daey Ouwens, C. (1993). *Wordt biomassa belangrijkste energiebron?* Duurzame Energie. 12: 10-13.

DE (1994). *Novem en ECN zullen zware klappen oplopen.* Duurzame Energie 9: 8.

DE (1999). *Groningen krijgt grootste vergistingsinstallatie ter wereld.* Duurzame Energie. 5: 40.

DE (2000). *Classificatiesysteem in de maak.* Duurzame Energie 2: 37.

DE (2002a). *Melkveebedrijf De Marke test installatie biomassavergisting.* Duurzame Energie: 38.

DE (2002b). *Overheid moet zekerheid en prikkels geven - Workshop Platform Bio-energie.* Duurzame Energie. 2: 39.

DE (2002c). *Melkveebedrijf De Marke test installatie biomassavergisting*. Duurzame Energie. 8: 38.

DE (2003b). *Stel tarieven MEP ten minste drie jaar van tevoren vast*. Duurzame Energie 5: 41.

E&MSpectrum (1993). *Biogas uit mest is geen kip met gouden eieren*. Energie- en Milieuspectrum 1: 10.

E&MSpectrum (1993). *Technieken gft-verwerking op een rijtje*. Energie- en Milieuspectrum: 14.

E&MSpectrum (1994). *Energiewereld likt de wonden*. Energie en Milieuspectrum 11: 28-31.

E&MSpectrum (1998). *Nederlandse beleid duurzame energie ambitious en duur*. Energie- en Milieuspectrum. 9: 5.

E&MT (1991). "Biogas van GFT-vergister samen met stortgas opgewerkt in Tilburg." Energie & Milieutechnologie 12(11/12): 10-11.

E&S, N. (1982). *Beperkte Mogelijkheden voor Energiegewassen in Nederlands*. Nieuwsbrief Energie & Samenleving. 7: 8.

E&S, N. (1982). *Het inkonsistente nederlandse energiebeleid*. Nieuwsbrief Energie & Samenleving. 7: 12.

E&S, N. (1983). *Biogasperspektief in de Landbouw*. Nieuwsbrief Energie & Samenleving 8(6).

ECN (1999). *Energie Verslag Nederland 1999*, Uitvoeringsnota Klimaatbeleid, Deel I: Binnelandse Maatregelen.

ECOFYS (2003). *Bio-energie van eigen bodem*. In opdracht van NOVEM.

Edquist, C (2001). *The systems of Innovation Approach and Innovation Policy: An account of the state of the art*. DRUID, Aalborg.

EZ (1995). *Derde Energie Nota - Duurzame energie*. Den Haag, Ministerie van Economische Zaken.

EZ, M. (2003). *Actieplan Biomassa: Samen werken aan bio-energie*.

Foxon, T. J., R. Gross, et al. (2005). *UK innovation systems for new and renewable energy technologies: drivers, barriers and systems failures*. Energy Policy 33(16): 2123-2137.

Haskoning (1991). *Conversietechnieken voor GFT-afval. Nationaal Onderzoekprogramma Hergebruik van Afvalstoffen (NOH)*. N. a. RIVM, Haskoning Ingenieurs bureau.

Haskoning (1992b). *Grootschalige scheiding en vergisting van huishoudekijk en bedrijfsafval*. In opdracht van Provinciaal Afvalverweijderingsbedrijf Zuid-Holland N.V. (PROAV).

Haskoning (1992c). *Onderzoek naar scheiding en vergisting van afval in Zuid-Oost Nederland.* In het kader van EWAB, in opdracht van NV Afvalverbranding Zuid-Nederland (AZN) en gesubsideerd van NOVEM.

Haskoning (1993). *Conversietechnieken voor GFT-afval - Ontwikkelingen in 1992.* In het kader van Nationaal Onderzoekprogramma Hergebruik van Afvalstoffen beheer en coordinatie bij NOVEM and RIVM.

Hoogwijk, M. (2004). *On the global and regional potential of renewable energy sources.* Chemistry. Utrecht, UU.

Hughes, T. P. (1983). *Networks of Power: Electrification in Western Society, 1880-1930.* Baltimore, The Johns Hopkins University Press.

IEA Task 29: *IEA Bio-energy Network on Socio-economics; Bioenergy: Anerobic Digestion.*

Jacobsson, S. and A. Bergek (2004). *Transforming the energy sector: the evolution of technological systems in renewable energy technology.* Ind Corp Change 13(5): 815-849.

Jacobsson, S. and A. Johnson (2000). *The diffusion of renewable energy technology: an analytical framework and key issues for research.* Energy Policy 28(9): 625-640.

Jacobsson, S. and A. Johnson (2001b). *The Emergence of a Growth Industry: A Comparative Analysis of the German, Dutch and Swedisch Wind Turbine Industries. Transformation and Development: Schumpeterian Perspectives (provisional title).* S. C. Metcalf, U. Heidelberg, Physica/Springer.

Jacobsson, S. and A. Johnson (2002). *Transforming the Energy Sector: The Evolution of Technological Systems in Renewable Energy Technology.* Gothenburg, IMIT and Department of Industrial Dynamics.

Janse, F. (1996a). *Gestage groei biomassaprojecten.* Duurzame Energie 3(6): 9.

Janse, F. (1996b). *GFT-vergistingsproject struikelt over voldoende aanvoer.* Duurzame Energie. 3: 12.

Janse, F. (1998). *Prijs biomassa remt ontwikkelingen.* Duurzame Energie,. 8: 12.

Johnson, A. and S. Jacobsson (2001a). *Inducement and Blocking Mechanisms in the Development of a New Industry: the Case of Renewable Energy Technology in Sweden.* Technology and the Market. *Demand, Users and Innovation.* R. Coombs, K. Green, A. Richards and V. Walsh. Cheltenham, Edwar Elgar Publishing Ltd: 89-111.

Kemp, R., J. Schot, et al. (1998). *Regime Shifts to Sustainability Through Processes of Niche Formation: The Approach of Strategic Niche Management.* Technology Analysis and Strategic Management 10(2): 175-195.

MilieuMagazine (2001). *Vergisten geniet de voorkeur,* Vakblad voor Milieumanagement. 12: 18.

Milieutechnologie, E. (1991). *Anaeroob vergistingsproces Biocel succesvol op praktijkschaal.* Energie & Milieutechnologie: 10.

Nes, W. J. (1988). *Doorgaan met mestvergisting*. Duurzame Energie. 2: 27-29.

Nes, W. J. (1989). *Wind en biogas leveren Deersum helft stroom*. Duurzame Energie. 11: 40-42.

NOVEM (1992). *Evaluatie van geintegreerd vergisten en verbranden van afval*. In het kader van Energiewinning uit Afval en Biomassa.

NOVEM (1998). *Lopende Projecten*. BioVisie. 9: 19.

Raven, R. P. J. M. (2004). *Implementation of manure digestion and co-combustion in the Dutch electricity regime: a multi-level analysis of market implementation in the Netherlands*. Energy Policy 32(1): 29-39.

Reumerman, P. (2004). *Personal Communication: Senior Consultant*, BTG biomass technology group B.V.

Sabatier, P. A. (1988). *An Advocacy Coalition Framework of Policy Change and the Role of Policy-Oriented Learning Therein*. Policy Sciences 21(2-3): 129-168.

Sabatier, P. A. (1998). *The advocacy coalition framework: revisions and relevance for Europe*. Journal of European Public Policy 5(1): 98-130.

Sabatier, P. A. and H. C. Jenkinssmith (1988). *Policy Change and Policy Oriented Learning - Exploring an Advocacy Coalition Framework - Introduction*. Policy Sciences 21(2-3): 123-127.

Sagar, A., D and J. Holdren, P. (2002). *Assessing the global energy innovation system: some key issues*. Energy Policy 30: 456-469.

Schot, J., R. Hoogma, et al. (1994). *Strategies for shifting technological systems - The case of automobile system*. Futures 26(10): 1060-1076.

Schot, J., R. Hoogma, et al. (1994). *Strategies for Shifting Technological Systems. The case of the automobile system*. Futures 26(10): 1060-1076.

Stromen (1999). *Nieuwe installatie maakt gft tot brandstof*. Stromen. 1.

Stromen (2003). *Energiewinning uit bermgras is alternatief*. Stromen. 5: 9.

Stromen (2004a). *VROM en LNV: eenvoudige regels voor mestvergisting*. Stromen 1(1): 7.

Stromen (2004d). *Tot vier keer hogere methaanopbrengst haalbaar: Nieuwe kans voor vergisting*." Stromen 19(11): 4.

TheBiomassSite Anaerobic Digestion.

TW (2004). *Vergisting hapert*. Technisch Weekblad 35(47): 15.

Unruh, G. C. (2000). *Understanding carbon lock-in*. Energy Policy 28(12): 817-830.

Unruh, G. C. (2002). *Escaping carbon lock-in*. Energy Policy 30(4): 317-325.

Utterback, J. M. (1994a). *Dominant Designs and Survival of the Firms. Mastering Dynamics of Innovation.* Boston, Massachusetts, Harvard Business School Press: 23-55.

Utterback, J. M. (1994b). *Innovation and Industrial Evolution. Mastering the Dynamics of Innovation.* Boston, Harvard Business School Press: 79-102.

Verbong, G. P. J., A. van Selm, et al. (2001). *Een kwestie van lange adem; De geschiednis van duurzame energie in Nederland.* Boxtel.

Vermaat, H. (1999). *Demonstratie-installatie vergist rest 'grijs' afval'.* Chemisch2Weekblad: 16-17.

Vos, d. R. C. J. (1994). *Reparatie van forse bezuiniging is nu eerste prioriteit; Energiewereld likt de wonden.* Energie & MilieuSpectrum 11: 28.

Wijland, G. v. (2004c). *Dik Tommel nieuwe voorzitter Platform Bio-Energie: 'Bio-energie moet zwaarwegend maatschappelijk belang worden.* Duurzame Energie 3: 14.

Zoeten, G. d., J. H. d. Zeeuw, et al. (1992). *Scheiden/vergistem reeel alternatief naast verbranden afval.* Energie & Milieutechnologie: 16-19.

Zoethout, T. (2004c). *Biogas voor boeren eindelijk aantrekkelijk.* Stromen 10(6): 4.

9 List of abbreviations

BSE	Resolution Subsidy Energy programme
CE	Centre for energy saving and environmental friendly technologies
CHP	Combined Heat and Power
ECN	Energy Research Centre of the Netherlands
EWAB	Energy production from waste and biomass
IMAG	Agrotechnology and Food Innovation
LCCA	Rural Coordination Commission for Waste Policy
LVK	Rural Sales Office
MEP	Environmental Quality Electricity Production
Ministry of EZ	Dutch Ministry of Economic Affairs
NMP	National Environmental Policy Plan
NOH	National Research programme for recycling of waste
NOVEM	Netherlands Agency for Energy and Environment
PDE	Dutch Office for Renewable Energies
REB	Regulating energy tax
SMB	Cooperation of Middle-Brabant County
TNO	Netherlands Organisation for Applied Scientific Research
TNO-MEP	TNO Environment, Energy and Process Innovation
VROM	Netherlands Ministry of Housing, Spatial Planning and the Environment

Emission Trading in Europe – First Experiences

Anke Eßer, Dominik Möst, Prof. Otto Rentz
Institute for Industrial Production (IIP), Universität Karlsruhe (TH), Germany

ABSTRACT: To meet the reduction targets set in the context of the Kyoto-Protocol, the European Union decided to implement a CO_2-emission trading system – the EU Emission Trading Scheme (ETS) – which started the 1.1.2005. Today, after more than six month of trading, a common market for EU-allowances begins to emerge. Prices as well as traded volumes increase continuously. Since the EU has chosen to integrate CDM and JI, the flexible mechanisms of the Kyoto-Protocol, into their trading scheme, EU-allowance prices may become decisive for the success of CDM / JI projects under the Kyoto-protocol. The paper in hand aims at analyzing the first experiences from emission trading in Europe. Therefore, the first part gives a general overview of emission trading platforms in Europe, providing for a comparison of allowances prices and traded volumes. In the last section the main determinants of EU-allowance prices are analysed.

1 Introduction

The Directive 2003/87/EC, establishing the European Emission Trading Scheme (ETS) for "greenhouse gas emission allowance trading within the Community" became effective on 1. January 2005. The actual trade with EU-allowances (EUA), each permitting the emission of 1 tonne CO_2, started the 1st March 2005. The directive aims at achieving the greenhouse gas emission reduction target of 8% (European Parliament and the Council of the European Union 2003), to which the Community committed itself by ratifying the Kyoto-Protocol. This reduction target of 8% was subdivided into national reduction targets (cp. table 1). The main features of the ETS are displayed in Table 1.

The ETS constitutes the world's largest emission trading scheme on company level; about 10.000 energy producing and energy-intensive units are affected (Graichen & Requate 2005). Companies receive a basic equipment of allowances for each trading period. At the end of the period they have to deliver the number of EU-allowances corresponding to their actual greenhouse gas emission. Companies emitting more than their basic equipment permits can either reduce their emissions, for example by investing in more efficient technology. Or they can buy additional allowances from companies not exhausting their limits.

To give companies more flexibility and cost-efficient means in how to fulfil their emission targets, and thus, to foster the transfer of environmentally sound technologies, the European Commission arranged for linking the flexible Kyoto-mechanisms Clean Development (CDM) and Joint Implementation (JI) to the ETS. The "Linking Directive" authorizes the conversion of project-based credits into an equal amount of EU-allowances.

Consequently, allowance prices have an influence on the realization of emission reduction projects. The possibility to invest in emission reduction projects, e.g. in industrializing countries, can be seen as an option (Spangardt & Meyer 2005), used to hedge against price risks. At low prices a company would by allowances on the market rather than invest in CDM and JI projects. Yet, if allowance prices are expected to rise considerably, the realisation of emission reduction projects becomes economically reasonable.

The first part of this paper gives a general overview of emission trading platforms in Europe, providing for a comparison of allowances prices and traded volumes. In the last section the main determinants of EU-allowance prices are analysed, permitting first conclusion concerning a possible influence on CDM / JI projects.

Table 1: National Emission Targets and Burden Sharing of the EU15 Member States

Member State	Emission Target [Mio. t CO_2]	Burden Sharing
Austria	7,8	-13%
Belgium	132,4	-7,5%
Denmark	54,9	-21%
Finland	77,2	0%
France	551,8	0%
Germany	960,8	-21%
Greece	133,8	+25%
Ireland	60,4	+13%
Italy	476,2	-6,5%
Luxemburg	7,8	-28%
Portugal	78,0	+27%
Sweden	75	+4%
Spain	333,4	+15%
United Kingdom	653,8	-12%
The Netherlands	198,4	-6%

Table 2: The main features of the European Emission Trading Scheme

Concept	"Cap and Trade" System
Time horizon	1st period: 2005-2007 2nd period: 2008-2012
Base	Carbon dioxide (CO_2) One allowance corresponds to the emission of one ton CO_2 equivalent
Participants	Operators of installation (Energy Production and energy-intensive installations) have to deliver a umber of EU-allowances corresponding to their greenhouse gas emission during a specific period. Any natural or legal person can participate in the trade.
Allocation	1st period: min. 95% free of charge 2nd period: min 90% free of charge Each member state has to issue a national allocation plan at least 3 month before the beginning of the period.

2 Overview of CO_2 Emission Trading Platforms in Europe

Since the Directive 2003/87/EC doesn't give any specification concerning the trading of EU-allowances, companies can choose whether they want to trade allowances via a broker ("over the counter") or for example via an exchange. The first allocation of EU-allowances took place the 28. February 2005. Ten days later, the European Energy Exchange (EEX) in Leipzig started its allowance spot auction. A market for forward transaction via brokers (OTC) had already emerged, before. At present about ten brokers, and seven European-wide exchanges on which EU-allowances or allowance-equivalents are traded can be identified (Laufkötter 2005). In the following, those platforms as well as their main characteristic shall be presented.

2.1 Over the Counter

By "Over the Counter" (OTC), trades via brokers (e.g. Natsource, Fichtner Consulting, or Trianel) are understood. Those brokers transact for operators or other market participants and charge a transaction fee in return. Characteristically fees charged for OTC-transaction are higher than fees charged by exchange operators. Since brokers bundle knowledge concerning emission trading, transaction costs can be reduced by assigning them to locate trading partners and carry out transactions. Hence, according to Laufkötter (2005), about 80% of all transactions are presently made by brokers. Point Carbon registered a share of 69% for OTC-trades (Point Carbon 2005a).

To provide transparency and to give an indication for market price development several OTC-price indicators are published, e.g.

- the Carbon Market Indicator, and
- the European Carbon Index.

The Carbon Market Indicator (CMI) is daily published by Point Carbon. It is measured by volume weighted assessment of information on market transaction between 7:30 am and 17:30 pm. Data is provided by active brokers (Point Carbon 2005c). The European Carbon Index (CO_2 Index) is released on a daily basis by the European Energy Exchange (EEX) in Leipzig as a reference price for CO_2-allowances. It is a volume weighted average price of OTC-deals in EU-allowances (EEX 2004).

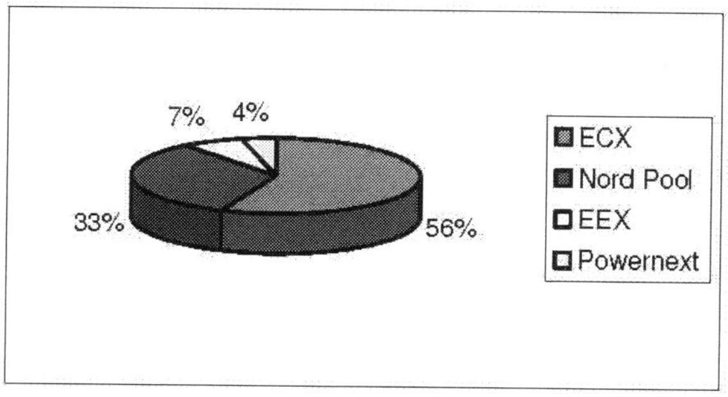

Figure 1: Share of major Europe based exchanges for EU-allowances (Point Carbon 2005a)

2.2 Exchanges

Besides OTC-deals an important proportion of transaction is made via exchanges. The seven European-based exchanges are the European Climate Exchange (ECX), Nord Pool, the European Energy Exchange (EEX), Powernext Carbon, Sendeco2, the Energy Exchange

Austria (EXAA), and New Values. Figure 1 shows their market shares (21. July 2005). (The market shares of Sendeco2, EXAA, and New Values are still too marginal compared to the four other exchanges.) In the following the four exchanges with the most important share of traded allowances, ECX, Nord Pool, EEX, and Powernext are introduced.

European Climate Exchange

The European Climate Exchange (ECX) is a joint venture of London's International Petroleum Exchange (IPE) and the Chicago Climate Exchange (CCX). On the ECX members have the possibility to trade spot as well as quarterly future contracts. (Not-members are allowed to trade as clients of members.) Those standardized contracts, the so-called Carbon Financial Instruments (ECX CFI), which are listed on the International Petroleum Exchange in London, have a size of 1,000 tonnes of CO_2. The electronic trading takes place daily from 8:00 am to 17:00 pm (BST) on a order driven continuous basis. At present (July 2005) 37 members are registered at IPE for participation at the ECX.

In June 2005 a press release was published disclosing ECX's ambition to merge with Powernext Carbon (International Emission Trading Association 2005).

Nord Pool

The Norwegian-based Power Exchange Nord Pool operates another market for EU-allowances, where standardized forward contracts, for 2005 - 2007, as well as spot contracts are listed. One contract complies with 1,000 EU-allowances, thus 1,000 t of CO_2. Trading takes place between 10:00 am and 15:30 pm (CET) on a continuous basis, via an electronic trading system. At the end of the day a "Daily Closing Price" is published. Besides the allowance spot market, Nord Pool also offers a clearing service for OTC-traded EU-allowances (Nord Pool, 2004a; Nord Pool, 2004b). At present, 59 members are authorized to participate in the market (July 2005).

European Energy Exchange

The 9th March 2005 the European Energy Exchange (EEX) in Leipzig started the first European spot auction for EU-allowances. Since, the EEX organizes daily spot auctions, determining equilibrium volumes and prices on a volume maximizing basis. The auctions run on the same time-tested trading and clearing system used for energy spot auctions. Every member, registered for the energy trading is authorized to participate in the allowance-spot-auction. At present 129 members are enrolled (July 2005) (EEX, 2005d; EEX, 2005c).

Besides the realization of the spot auctions, the EEX publishes the European Carbon Index (cp. Chapter 1.1.1), and the implementation of a market for CO_2-emission futures is planned in the course of the year 2005 (Laufkötter 2005).

Powernext Carbon

Powernext Carbon is the EU-allowance exchange launched by the French power exchange Powernext, in partnership with the banking house Caisse des Dépôts, and the pan-European stock exchange Euronext. The EU-allowance spot market started the 24 June 2005. Since, it is operating every day form 10:00 am to 2:00 (CET) pm on a order driven continuous basis (Powernext et al. 2005). The number of its active members amounts to 13 (July 2005).

3 Evolution of volumes and prices for EU-allowances

The EU Emission Trading Scheme is the largest market for CO_2-allowances in the world[17]. Since January 2004 about 39 Million t of CO_2-equivalents[18] were exchanged, most of them since the official start of the scheme in January 2005. As shown in Figure 1, the European Climate Exchange has the highest market share, followed by Nord Pool, the European Energy Exchange, and Powernext. The total amount of EU-allowances traded at the ECX between the 28.04.2005 and 29.06.2005 amounts to 7,018,000 pieces. For comparison, 346,308 EU-allowances were exchanged at the EEX during the same period (also cp. Figure 2). 2005-allowances represent about 90% of the volume traded. 2006 allowances make up about 6% and 2007-allowances about 4% (Lecocq & Capoor, 2005). (Those shares have been deduced from the EU-allowance future trades.)

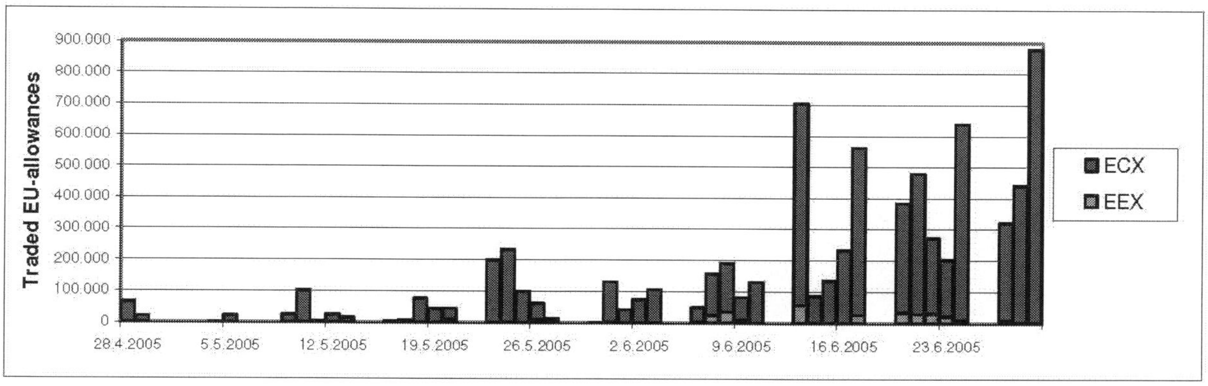

Figure 2: Trading volumes at the European Climate Exchange and the European Energy Exchange (EEX, 2005b; Chicago Climate Exchange, 2005)

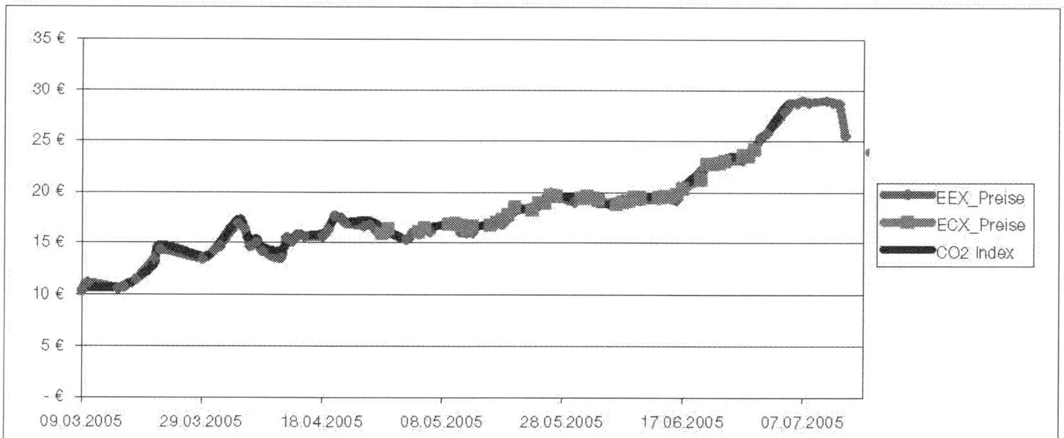

Figure 3: Evolution of EU-allowance prices (EEX, 2005a; EEX, 2005b; Chicago Climate Exchange, 2005)

Prices have risen considerably since the beginning of the EU emission trading from about 10 Euros to more than 25 Euros (cp. Figure 3). The average prices of the EU-allowances traded on the ECX, and the EEX as well as OTC (reference: European Carbon Index) since the

[17] There exists 3 other trading schemes for green house gas emission trading, for example the UK ETS (cp. Eßer 2004), the New South Wales trading scheme and the Chicago Climate Exchange (Lecocq & Capoor, 2005).

[18] The cumulative volume of allowances exchanged adds up to 56 Mio. t. CO_2. To compare, the total budget of EU-allowances distributed whole Europe amounts to more than 6,000 Mio. t of CO_2.

Capoor (2005) reason that this is due to the homogeneity of the asset and the contracts traded. Prices for EU-allowance-futures for 2006 and 2007 have about the same evolution and differ only slightly from those for 2005 (cp. Figure 4 and 5). This could be explained by the fact that banking as well as borrowing is allowed within the ETS.

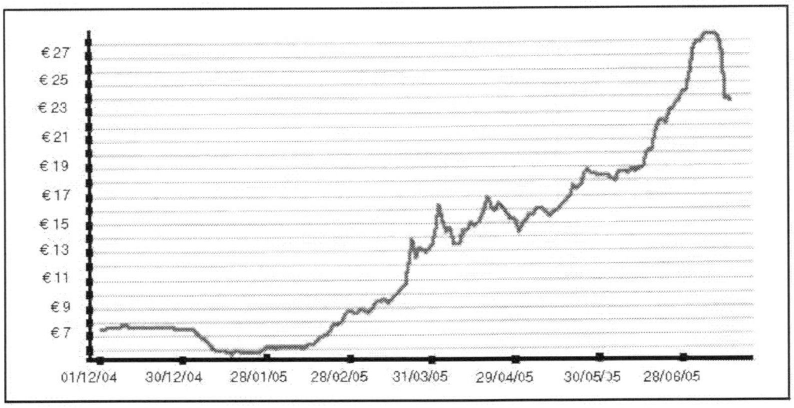

Figure 4: Historic prices for EU-allowance futures for 2006 (Point Carbon 2005b)

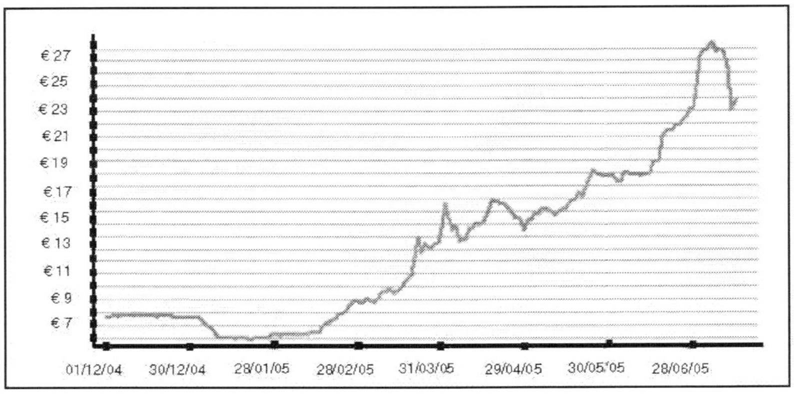

Figure 5: Historic prices for EU-allowance-futures for 2007 (Point Carbon 2005b)

As stated above credits granted for CDM and JI projects can be converted one-to-one into EU-allowances. Yet the average price of Certified Emission Reductions (CER) from CDM-projects, and Emission Reduction Units (ERU) from JI-projects, between January 2004 and April 2005 was 4.67 Euros respectively 5.01 Euros.[19] This imbalance can only partly be explained by the higher risks buyers have to assume buying project related allowances. According to Lecocq and Capoor (2005) it is more likely, that the current price for EU-allowances "might still not be representative of the supply / demand equilibrium." For this reason, the main determinants of the EU allowances prices shall be discussed in the following section, in order to analyse EU-allowance prices

[19] Exchange rate 1 USD = 0,83 Euros (28.07.2005)

4 Analysis of EU-allowance prices

There exist various factors, which have an influence on EU-allowance price development (Schafhausen 2005). In this chapter the factors

- the gas/oil prices,
- the quantity of liquid allowances, and
- the number of market participants

shall be discussed.

Gas and Oil prices

The factor most frequently referred to as one of the key determinants for high allowance prices is the gas respectively the oil price. Comparing the evolution of the IPE Gas Oil Afternoon Marker with the CO_2-Index of the last month (cp. Figure 6), a correlation seems assumable. In fact, the coefficient of correlation amounts to 0.77, which indicates a fairly strong positive correlation. Especially a strong rise in oil / gas prices, like it occurred at the beginning of July 2005 appears to be followed by an at least equal increase in EU-allowance prices. This interdependency can be explained by the need of utilities to hedge against a potential increase in costs due to higher CO_2-emission. This increase can be traced back to a potential switch from gas to coal, which results in an increase in CO_2-emissions. Consequently the demand for EU-allowances augments. Thus the currently high allowance price can, to some extent, be explained by the high oil / gas prices.

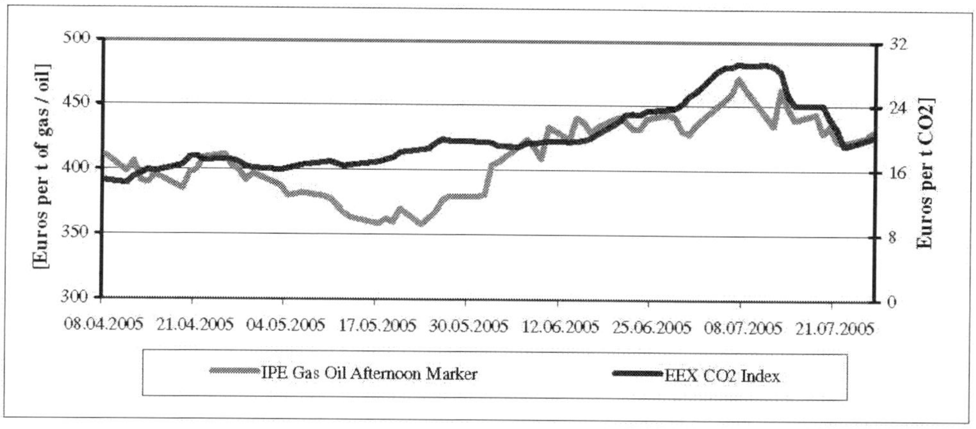

Figure 3: Comparison of the Evolution of gas/oil prices and EU-allowance prices (EEX, 2005a; International Petrolium Exchange, 2005)

The quantity of liquid EU-allowances

The amount of allowances emitted or rather the amount of allowances on the market is a crucial factor for the evolution of EU-allowance prices. In case of shortage, allowance prices rise; in case of a stark backlog of supply, allowances prices are rather low.

Accordingly, the design of the national allocation plans (NAPs), in which the Member States define the reduction path for the industries participating in the ETS, has an important influence on allowance prices. If emission targets are rather stringent, companies might have difficulties to achieve their predetermined targets. As a result the demand in EU-allowances augments and consequently allowance prices rise. At present, most Member States published rather lenient NAPs. Thus the comparatively high prices cannot be explained by an over-demand for EU-allowances due to strict national reduction paths.

Besides the NAPs, the quantity of credits accorded for CDM and JI projects is another factor having an crucial influence on the amount of allowances on the market. The more projects are carried out, the more credits might be converted into EU-allowances. This could, on the one hand, decrease the demand at the various exchanges. On the other hand, it could increase the liquidity of the market. Yet, due to regulatory uncertainties and the high transaction costs[20] an only marginal number of credits has actually been granted so far (Lecocq & Capoor 2005).

Finally, it has often been predicted that as soon as the market for EU-allowances is established, a considerably amount of EU-allowances from east European countries would flood the market and beat down prices. Up to now, no such phenomenon took place (Lecocq and Capoor 2005). None the less, once the eastern countries have built up functioning national trading facilities and gain knowledge about the ETS, the liquidation of a great number of EU-allowances, set free due to the decline of the east European industry, should be expected.

The number of participants in the EU-allowance market

Even though the number of market participants is continually rising, it seems that "only a limited number of companies from a very small number of countries (essentially the UK, Germany, France, Belgium, and the Netherlands) have participated so far in the market." Especially the eastern European Member States showed little interest in EU emission trading until now (see above).

Since a limited number of participants is one of the key indicators for a illiquid market, this might indicate, that the prices for EU-allowances are still not representative.

5 Conclusion

Since the beginning of the European Emission Trading Scheme in January 2005 a substantial European market for CO_2-allowances is developing. Although trading is basically still taking place "over the counter" the importance of exchange grows. Trading volumes increase continuously and a uniform price for EU-allowances has emerged.

The price for EU-allowances is rather high, in all probability due to high oil respectively gas prices. Hence a positive effect on the number of realized emission reduction projects under the Kyoto-protocol might be expected. However, there subsists several indicators that suggest that the price for EU-allowances is not yet representative, and a diminution should be expected.

First of all, there is an spread of more than 10 Euros between the price for project credits and EU-allowances, which can hardly be explained by higher risks. Moreover the number of market participants is still quite limited. Particularly the participation of eastern European countries in the Trading Scheme is still low. Yet an increasing participation can be assumed over the next several month, probably having a sustainable influence on allowance price development.

Recapitulatoryly can be retained, that today's high allowance prices might have a positive impact on CDM / JI project realization. Since allowance prices are expected to come down, this effect will probably not be sustainable.

---

[20] With a price of 3 Euros / CER Michaelowa (2005) calculated a required number of 20.000 CERs to cover the transaction costs.

6 References

Chicago Climate Exchange. *ECX hits new record and breaks the 7 Million tonnes bar*. 2005. 29-6-2005.

EEX. *Terms and Conditions for the Determination of a CO_2 Index as well as Formal Obligation for Reporters*. European Energy Exchange. 2004.

EEX. *EEX CO_2 Index*. European Energy Exchange. 2005a.

EEX. *EEX Emissionsmarkt*. European Energy Exchange. 2005b.

EEX. *EEX successfully starts Trading of Allowances*. European Energy Exchange. 2005c. 9-3-2005c.

EEX. *Transition provisions regarding trading in EU emission allowances contracts on EEX*. European Energy Exchange. 2005d.

Eßer A (2004). *Die Konzeption eines Systems handelbarer Umweltrechte für den Straßengüterverkehr in ökologisch besonders sensiblen Regionen,* Discussion –paper 1/04. Institut für Wirtschaftspolitik und Wirtschaftsforschung (IWW), Universität Karlsruhe (TH)

European Parliament and the Council of the European Union (2003), *Directive 2003/87/EC of the European Parliament and of the Council of 13 October 2003 establishing a scheme for greenhouse gas emission allowances trading within the Community and amending Council Directive 96/61/EC*, Official Journal of the European Union 32-46

Graichen P, Requate T (2005), *Der steinige Weg von der Theorie in die Praxis des Emissionsrechtehandels: Die Eu-Richtlinie zum CO_2-Emissionsrechtehandel und ihre nationale Umsetzung*, Perspektiven der Wirtschaftspolitik 6: 41-56

International Emission Trading Association. *Joint emissions platfom planned*. 2005. 24-6-2005.

International Petrolium Exchange. *IPE Gas Oil Historical Data*. 2005.

Laufkötter S (2005), *Börsengeschäfte mit heißer Luft - Spotmarktgeschäfte für den CO_2-Emissionshandel*, EW 104: 24-26

Lecocq F, Capoor K (2005), *State and Trends of the Carbon Market 2005*, World Bank,

Michaelowa A (2005), *Clean Development Mechnism und Joint Implementation, in Emissionshandel - Ökonomische Prinzipien, rechtliche Regelungen und technische Lösungen für den Klimaschutz*, ed. Lucht M and Spangardt G, Springer, Berlin, Heidelberg p 137-152

Nord Pool. *Contract Specification: EU Allowances (EUA) - Trading and Clearing Services at Nord Pool*. Nord Pool ASA. 2004a.

Nord Pool. *Trading Rules for Trading of Allowances at Nord Pool ASA*. Nord Pool ASA. 2004b.

Point Carbon. *Carbon Market Daily Vol 1 Issue 123*. 2005a.

Point Carbon. *Historic Prices for EUAs 2005 - 2007*. 2005b.

Point Carbon. *Price Information - methodology*. 2005c.

Powernext et al. *Powernext Carbon "An organised market to fight climate change..."*. Powernext, Caisse des Dépôts, and Euronext. 2005.

Schafhausen F (2005), *Politische Umsetzung von Kioto in der EU und in Deutschland, in Emissionshandel - Ökonomische Prinzipien, rechtliche Regelungen und technische Lösungen für den Klimaschutz*, ed. Lucht M and Spangardt G, Springer, Berlin Heidelberg p 51-85

Spangardt G, Meyer J (2005), *Risikomanagement im Emissionshandel, in Emissionshandel - Ökonomische Prinzipien, rechtliche Regelungen und technische Lösungen für den Klimaschutz*, ed. Lucht M and Spangardt G, Springer, Berlin, Heidelberg p 219-232

Promoting Renewable Energy through CDM Capacity Building Programmes: The Case of Some ASEAN Countries

Axel Michaelowa, Dang Hong Hanh, Soren Varming
Hamburg Institute of International Economics, Germany and Econ Denmark

ABSTRACT: Renewable energy projects make up the majority of projects under the Kyoto Protocol's Clean Development Mechanism (CDM) worldwide. CDM capacity building is in full swing in the larger and economically relatively advanced ASEAN countries. Overall, more than 17 million € have been spent in over 20 multi- and bilateral programmes. After starting with awareness raising and institution building, since 2003 support of project development is the key focus. This may mobilize renewable energy CDM projects if they are almost commercially attractive, such as biomass waste-based power plants from agriculture (palm oil waste, bagasse and rice husk). Over 20 renewable energy CDM projects from ASEAN have already full official CDM documentation whereas up to 100 projects are under development. Targeted capacity building for renewable energy might be able to lead to a higher success rate for such projects in the CDM registration process than would currently be likely.

1 Introduction to the CDM situation in ASEAN

The Clean Development Mechanism (CDM) under the Kyoto Protocol allows industrialized countries to generate greenhouse gas emission credits (Certified Emission Reductions, CERs) through emission reductions achieved by projects in developing countries (commonly called host countries). Through the CDM which is overseen by an international CDM Executive Board (EB), the industrialized countries can reduce the costs of fulfilling their emission commitments while assisting developing countries to achieve sustainable development. However, harnessing of the CDM requires building the capacity of government agencies and the private sector to manage and develop CDM project activities. A host country can only participate in the CDM if it has ratified the Kyoto Protocol and notified a Designated National Authority (DNA) to the Secretariat of the UN Framework Convention on Climate Change (UNFCCC). The ASEAN member countries (Brunei, Cambodia, Indonesia, Laos, Malaysia, Myanmar, Philippines, Singapore, Thailand, and Vietnam) show significant differences in both CDM project development and in establishing the related policy and institutional framework. Table 1 summarizes the institutional situation for the CDM in ASEAN.

The private sector plays a key role in implementing CDM projects. The following analysis is taken from CAP SD et al. (2005).

In Malaysia, the driving force – to date – behind the development of CDM project ideas appears to have been local corporations. Major palm oil producers such as Felda, Golden Hope, and ISI have been relatively active participants in the project development market. While there have been third party developers, they have less traction in Malaysia than in either the Philippines or Thailand, though one local firm (Bumibiopower) has engaged the CDM through biomass project development opportunities.

Table 1: CDM institutions in ASEAN

Country	Kyoto Protocol ratified	DNA notified to UNFCCC	Published DNA procedures	Necessary CDM conditions fulfilled	Supportive CDM framework
Brunei	-	-	-	-	-
Cambodia	22 August 2002	November 2003	-	Yes	Yes
Indonesia	3 December 2004	-	Yes	-	Partially
Lao PDR	6 February 2003	November 2003	-	Yes	-
Malaysia	4 September 2002	May 2003	Yes	Yes	Yes
Myanmar	13 August 2003	-	-	-	-
Philippines	20 November 2003	September 2004	-	Yes	Yes
Singapore	-	-	-	-	-
Thailand	28 August 2002	June 2004	-	Yes	Partially
Vietnam	25 September 2002	December 2003	Yes	Yes	Yes
Total ASEAN	**8**	**6**	**3**	**6**	**4**

Source: data from UNFCCC website, status July 27, 2005 and personal communication

[1] DNA has been set up by ministerial decree in July 2005

In Indonesia, up to now multinationals have been very visible but the picture starts to change. Early proponents of CDM projects in Indonesia have been led by the American multinational, Unocal, seeking to gain value for its existing and prospective geothermal portfolio in the country. Other major energy multinationals, such as ChevronTexaco, Statkraft and Sumitomo, have also been engaged in early stage Indonesia projects, though none have yet been fully developed. There are other prospective projects involving local developers in Indonesia similar to the Malaysian situation, but they have not been as high profile. As Indonesia only ratified the Kyoto Protocol in the summer of 2004, the extent to which this paradigm will remain dominant is still to be determined.

Similarly to Indonesia, in Vietnam large flagship projects outside the renewable energy sector have been done by multinationals (ConocoPhillips and the Japan-Vietnam Oil Corporation).

In Thailand and the Philippines, the driving force would appear to be third party, smaller scale project developers such as the Clean Technologies Thailand, the UK project development firm Bronzeoak and Philippine BioSciences - a US-Philippine company.

2 Renewable energy in the CDM worldwide and in ASEAN

Renewable energy is currently the leading CDM project type worldwide when it comes to the number of projects (see Figure 1).

However, the share of CERs forecast for renewable energy projects is much smaller than the share of projects (see Figure 2) due to a low CER generation rate per project.

ASEAN countries so far only have a limited amount of renewable energy project documents in the official validation and methodology development processes (see Table 2). This may be due to the fact that CDM revenue is not yet taken into account by potential equity investors or loan providers despite generating free cash flow that can be readily applied to debt service obligations. For a wind project of 100 MW, equity investment needs could thus be reduced by 20% at CER prices of 7 € (CAP SD et al., 2005). Only a minority of energy developers and an even smaller percentage of bankers and equity providers are able to evaluate the CER revenue stream; thus there is a strong need for CDM capacity building.

From those 23 proposed project activities originated 6 approved methodologies. In Thailand, the first project in the region whose methodology was approved by the CDM Executive Board was a rice husk IPP, called AT Biopower. AT Biopower will begin operations in early 2005 as a 22 MW facility, with the potential of expansion to 88 MW, over time. The Korat tapioca starch factory has recently installed a 5 MW power plant fuelled by methane from anaerobic decomposition of the wastewater. The baseline methodology has been recommended for approval by the Methodology Panel of the EB but due to the EB's aim to consolidate all methodologies for biomass-based electricity generation for the grid, it has not yet been officially published.

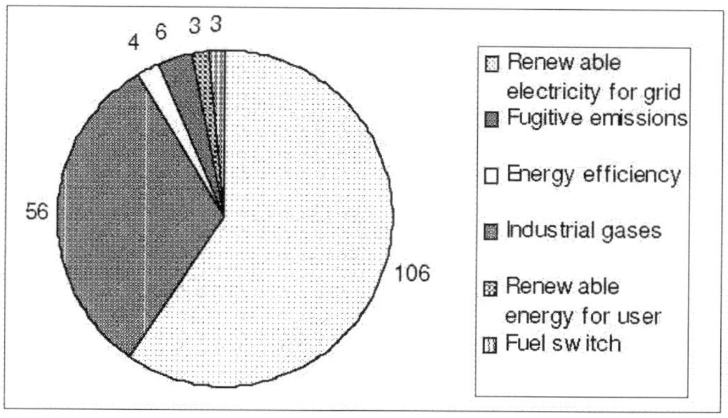

Source: data from UNFCCC website, status July 27, 2005

Figure 1: Share of renewable energy projects in total submitted and registered CDM projects

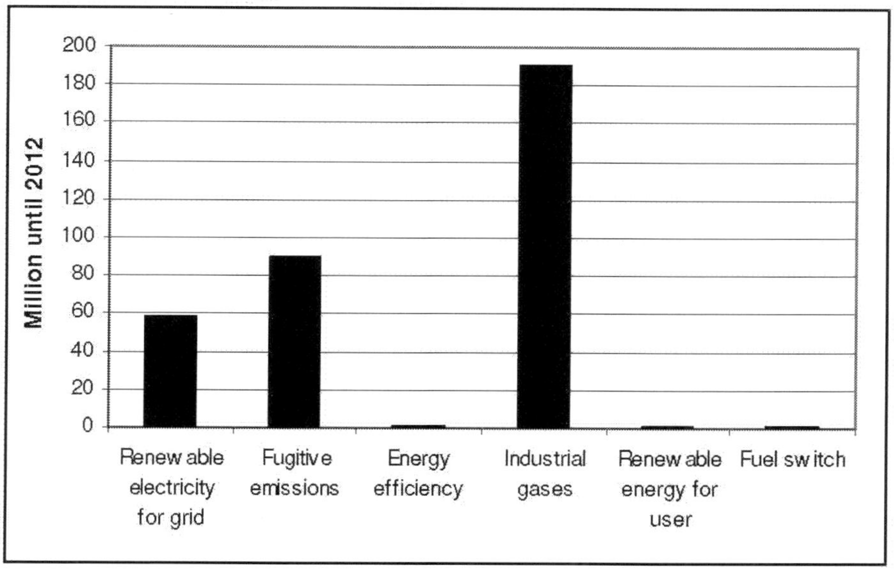

Source: data from UNFCCC website, status July 27, 2005

Figure 2: Renewable energy CER generation from submitted and registered projects

Besides the projects officially submitted for validation and baseline methodology approval, there is a high number of "grey" projects in different stages of development. It is difficult to keep track of them but an overview is attempted in Table 3

Beyond the Korat project, Clean Technologies Thailand has developed a pipeline of 17 waste to energy projects within both the cassava starch processing and burgeoning ethanol production business (Plevin & Donelly, 2004; Beltran et al., 2005). All of these projects are being undertaken in a project finance structure, rather than with existing corporate sponsors. The problem with those projects is that most of them are already commercially attractive without the CDM at IRRs ranging between 13 and 21% (see also). Thus it is unclear whether they will pass the additionality test. A third significant development - the Mitr Phol rubberwood waste project - was undertaken by the underlying company in an on-balance sheet fashion, but seems to have stalled since early negotiations.

In the Philippines, Bronzeoak has made significant progress in developing CDM projects for bagasse waste on the island of Negros and in other locales. Philippine BioSciences has teamed up with CleanThai and is developing five CDM projects on industrial waste streams, most notably in energy recovery from sugarcane liquor wastes from a distillery in Tarlac Province.

Table 2: Overview on project activities in the validation and baseline methodology pipeline (until 27July 2005)

Project types	Total project type	No. of submitted project activities/ ASEAN country					
		Cambodia	Indonesia	Malaysia	Philippines	Thailand	Vietnam
Solar energy	1	-	1	-	-	-	-
Biomass energy	7	1	-	3	-	3	-
Landfill gas to energy	4	1	1	1	1	1	-
Methane capture from liquid waste for heat and electricity generation	9	-	-	1	6	1	1
Production of bio-fuel for use in transportation	2	-	1	-	-	1	-
Total	**23**	**2**	**3**	**5**	**7**	**6**	**1**

Table 3: Sector distribution of renewable energy CDM project ideas from ASEAN countries

Country	**Biomass/waste**	**Hydro**	**Geothermal**	**LFG**	**Wind**	**Total**
Cambodia	2	1	0	1	0	**4**
Indonesia	12	3	8	3	0	**26**
Malaysia	8	1	0	3	0	**12**
Philippines	6	1	1	1	2	**11**
Thailand	20	0	0	0	0	**20+**
Vietnam	2	7	1	3	2	**15**
Total ASEAN	**50**	**13**	**10**	**11**	**4**	**88**

Sources: UNFCCC CDM website, presentations at South East Asia Greenhouse Gas Market Forum October 2004, presentations at Workshop on Financing Modalities of the CDM, Jakarta, June 2005, personal communication Agus Sari, DNV. Overlaps cannot be excluded.

3 Capacity Building Programmes in ASEAN and their impact on renewable energy projects

ASEAN has been targeted by a high number of capacity building programmes. This is due to the fact that the countries offer a high CDM potential and are generally perceived to have a relatively high education level, meaning that initial capacity building efforts would readily be disseminated. Table 4 summarizes the different activities.

Table 4: CDM capacity building in ASEAN

Country	Multilateral donor programmes	Bilateral donor programmes	Budget (million €)	Duration	Aims
Brunei	-	-	-	-	-
Cambodia	CD4CDM, CF Assist, EU ProEco	Australia, Japan	2.0	2002-ongoing	DNA support and PDD development
Indonesia	ADB (2), UNIDO, GGFR	Australia, Denmark, Germany, Japan Netherlands	6.5	2000-ongoing	DNA support and PDD development
Lao PDR	EU ProEco	Netherlands	0.2	2004-ongoing	DNA support
Malaysia	UNDP, UNIDO	Denmark	2.0	2001-ongoing	DNA support and PDD development
Myanmar	-	-	-	-	-
Philippines	CD4CDM, UNIDO	Japan, Netherlands	2.3	2001-ongoing	DNA support and PDD development
Singapore	-	-	-	-	-
Thailand	UNIDO	Denmark, Japan	2.2	2001-ongoing	DNA support and PDD development
Vietnam	CD4CDM, UNIDO, EU ProEco	Australia, Germany	1.2	2001-ongoing	DNA support and PDD development
Regional	EU, World Bank	-	0.6	2003-2004	Information sharing
Total ASEAN	**10**	**14**	**17330**		

Sources: programme websites, personal communication Agus Sari. World Bank National Strategy Studies are listed under bilateral programmes according to the relevant donor. Budget figures are estimates by the author as most smaller programmes do not publish their budgets; for more detailed information on specific programmes see Michaelowa (2004).

There are three distinct phases of capacity building. Between 2000 and 2002, overview studies and awareness-raising workshops dominated. From 2002 to 2004, DNA building took the centre stage while from 2003 concrete PDD support programmes started to develop. While some donors (Australia, Germany) do not aim to generate CERs for their compliance, Denmark, Japan and the Netherlands want to pave the way to acquire CERs. Especially the Danish programmes are very much targeted and try to connect capacity building with CER generation through project development facilities. In Thailand however, only capacity building was requested by theThai side which led to a unilateral continuation of the project development on the Danish side. Recent capacity building also tend to focus more on raising the CDM awareness of the financial sector.

4 Case studies Indonesia, Vietnam and Cambodia

4.1 Indonesia

Indonesia is by far the largest country in ASEAN. It has a wide range of attractive renewable energy options – geothermal with an estimated potential of more than 9 GW, biomass and hydro. The financial crisis in 1997 and the ensuing political turmoil relegated climate change issues to a back seat. Only in 1999 some interest re-emerged and was catalysed through the Climate Change Programme of the German Agency for Technical Cooperation (GTZ). Due to a long history of close collaboration the links to the Ministry of Environment are strong and the idea of a National Strategy Study (NSS) for the energy sector was quickly endorsed. The NSS was finalised in September 2001 (State Ministry of the Environment, 2001). It estimated the annual CER potential from renewable energy as follows[21]:

- Geothermal: 139 million
- Biomass: 23 million, of which 7 million in palm oil mills, 3.5 million in pulp and paper plants and 2 million in tapioca starch plants
- Large hydropower: 10 million
- Small hydropower: 5 million

The NSS accorded a high priority to small hydro and biomass waste use for energy production in pulp and paper, starch plants and palm oil plant while standard hydro was accorded medium and geothermal low priority due to its high costs. An analysis of a empty fruit bunch-fired 10 MW power plant by Institut Teknologi Bandung (2002) shows that palm oil waste electricity projects can be very attractive, reaching IRRs of about 20%. This of course makes additionality of such projects questionable. The overall technical CER potential of palm-oil waste to energy projects in Indonesia is around 10 million p.a. (see Table 5).

Table 5: Palm-oil waste-to-energy based technical CDM potential in Indonesia

Type of waste	Amount of waste produced in Indonesia	Possible electric capacity	CERs from fossil electricity replacement	CERs from methane combustion
Empty fruit bunches	11 million t	240 MW	1.3 million	-
Liquid waste (POME)	25 million m^3	190 MW	1.1 million	8 million
Total		**430 MW**	**2.4 million**	**8 million**

Sources: Estimates based on production of 10 million tonnes of crude palm oil and data from Institut Teknologi Bandung (2002), data from Matsushita Electric Industrial Co et al. (2003). 50% of Empty Fruit Bunches are assumed to be used in current palm oil mill boilers. The baseline electricity grid emission factor is assumed to be 750 g CO_2/kWh.

[21] These estimates were done on the basis of energy demand forecasts for 2025 and the year 2000 emission factors of the Java-Bali grid. They are thus likely to be on the high end.

During the NSS process, the association of geothermal producers played a very active role while other renewable energy project developers were largely absent. However, two geothermal projects that had been contemplated to develop CDM documentation were unable to go ahead. In the case of the Wayang Windu project which had already been allocated a purchase contract under the Dutch CERUPT initiative, a change in ownership led to a cancellation of the CDM development. Currently, it is attempted to revive this project. The problem with geothermal projects is that the gap between their electricity generation costs and those of fossil power plants is unlikely to be closed by the CER revenues. The geothermal plants currently operating in Indonesia were only built due to high-price power purchase agreements concluded under corrupt circumstances in the last years of the Suharto era. Of course, this means that additionality of these projects is easy to prove.

After the completion of the NSS, German capacity building focused on DNA support while the Netherlands were trying to negotiate a Bilateral CER Purchase Agreement. At first, 5 million CERs were envisaged but due to the lack of attractive project proposals, the volume was scaled down to 2 million. The Danish CDM Project Development Facility was launched in July 2005. It aims to acquire 5 million CERs; the first tender for project ideas starts in October 2005. Discussions at the inception workshop showed that there is high interest in biomass residue-based projects, particularly the palm oil sector. Surprisingly, the small hydro sector has so far not been able to mobilize any CDM project.

4.2 Vietnam

In regard to the functions of DNA and relevant CDM institutions, Vietnam is quite ahead in the region. One of the main reason is that the country has participated quite early in the regional mitigation assessment projects, i.e: Asia Least-cost Greenhouse Gas Abatement Strategy – (ALGAS) and Promotion of Renewable Energy, Energy Efficiency and Greenhouse Gas Abatement (PREGA) both executed by the ADB. From 1999 to 2004, the NSS was conducted by the World Bank and funded by the Government of Australia. Although the outputs of the final report are not very updated in some context, the project has contributed considerably to improve the awareness of public actors, especially at the central government level on the CDM issues. The current on-going capacity building projects (CD4CDM, CDM EU ProEco) have been contributing to strengthening the country's CDM institutional structures and promoting the activeness of other non-public stakeholders. the dominant targeted audience of these capacity building programmes so far is public sector which implies the weakness of the private sector acting as project-based stakeholders under the CDM. The Prime Minister's Directive on CDM is planned tobe promulgated in the end of 2005. This will be important in term of co-ordinating and promoting CDM activities at the national level.

Vietnam has a medium CDM potential in the areas of renewable energy (see Table 6). Up to March 2005, 14 renewable energy projects with a total annual CER potential of 0.7 million has been compiled in the list of 25 PINs by CD4CDM (NOCCOP, 2005).

Similar to Indonesia, no small hydro project in Vietnam has been mobilised into a CDM project yet, although the country has experience in exploiting small hydro power and the government has a policy of promoting micro hydro. Some 40 small hydro stations (1 to 10 MW) have been constructed, with a total capacity of 70 MW, representing only about 3 % of the potential. For 100 kW to 1 MW plants (500 potential sites), 10 MW of a potential 200 MW (5 % of potential) has been developed (Nguyen Tien Long, 2004). The barriers to develop the small hydroelectricity stations as CDM projects may be due to the general sensitiveness to financial variables of hydro powers (relatively high up-front costs and long payback period) and the difficulty in bundling small projects to be commercially attractive under the CDM.

Table 6: Estimated renewable energy potential and current use in Vietnam

Sources	Potential (MW)	Used (MW)	Located
Small hydro connected to grid	400-600	60	North & Central
Independent small hydropower	300-600	20	North & Central
Minihydro	90-150	30-75	North & Central
Biomass	250-400	50	South & Central
Geothermal	50-200	0	Central
Wind power		0.4	Central & Islands
Solar		0.2	South
Total	1,090-1,950	160-215	

Source: Vietnam NSS, 2004

Vietnam is a predominantly agrarian nation. Consequently, biomass residues from agriculture are relatively abundant in both quantity and type (see Table 7). Biomass from rice husk is peculiar rich given the position of the country as the 3rd largest rice exporter in the world.

Table 7: Potential of biomass for electricity generation

Type of biomass	**Main biomass produced (million tons)**	**Available biomass (million tons)**	**Estimated potential of electricity generation (MW)**
Rice husk	6.6	2.5	70-150
Bagasse	5.5	4.6	150-200
Wood residues	0.48	-	5
Wastes and other biomass	-	-	30-50

Source: Nguyen Duc Cuong, 2004

Until present, biomass is mostly gathered and used locally and in traditional way. The National Program on bio-fuels for 2005-2020 is under construction. Unfortunately, no linking and integration with CDM potential have been mentioned in the draft yet. To date, only one rice husk power plant in Tien Giang province is developed into PDD with about 55,000 CER per year (NOCCOP, 2005). Given the availability of the methodology for a similar rice husk project in Thailand, the lack of project developers in the country and small scale of milling facilities can be the explanation for their behind in developing such a project type. Currently, there are 42 medium to large scale sugar manufactures in Vietnam, but only 3 of them supply surplus power to the electricity grid with total capacity is up to 100 MW.

So far two wind farm projects in two islands of Vietnam (Ly Son and Phu Quy) have been developed into PDDs by local experts based on the pre-feasibility studies of the Institute of Energy. However, the baseline calculation and other technical aspects are not credible in the eyes of international experts. For a long term, the lacking wind data in the country (ADB, 2004) and high investment costs will continue being a barrier to promote the utilisation of wind energy in Vietnam.

Generally, limited reliable project financing and lack of knowledgeable local experts will be constraints to promote renewable energy via CDM in Vietnam.

The trends of developing CDM in renewable energy and the fact of CDM capacity building in Vietnam show that to promote renewable projects under the CDM, the synergy of different government priorities, programmes is needed. Further capacity building should focus on facilitating private stakeholders and sectoral pre-feasibility studies. For example, a demonstration of bundling small hydro powers that are highly replicable could be more illustrative for investors to make investment decisions.

4.3 Cambodia

Cambodia is one of the few least developed countries that have set up a DNA. This is due to the fact that it has virtually been swamped with capacity building funds (see Table 4); in terms of CDM capacity funding per € of GDP, Cambodia must be the world leader. The different programmes have led to the setup of an effective DNA that has high human capacity.

However, the virtual absence of foreign investment in Cambodia makes it extremely difficult to develop actual projects. While a 1.5 MW rice husk power plant has actually been submitted for validation, the pipeline of a dozen small hydro projects drawn up by the DNA has so far not found any interested investor. A workshop with hotel owners in the tourist boom town of Siem Reap showed that despite good financial data, low technical risk and a nice bundling potential, the use of solar thermal power was not attractive to the hotel owners.

5 Conclusions

There has been intense CDM capacity building in the larger and economically relatively advanced ASEAN countries during the last five years. Overall, more than 17 million € have been spent in over 20 multi- and bilateral programmes. While in the early stages, they focused on awareness raising and institution building, since 2003 programmes to support PDD development have gained importance. These programmes have generated some controversy when the donor linked capacity building funds to project development with the aim to generate CERs. It remains to be seen whether the current tender programmes mobilize renewable energy CDM projects but they are likely to do so if the projects are almost commercially attractive. This is the case for biomass waste-based power plants from agriculture (palm oil waste, bagasse and rice husk), less so for hydropower. Over 20 renewable energy CDM projects have already been submitted for validation and development of new baseline methodologies whereas up to 100 projects are under development. Targeted capacity building for renewable energy might be able to lead to a higher success rate for such projects in the CDM registration process than currently likely. The key is to make financial institutions understand that CER revenues enhance the creditworthiness of a project and thus are more eager to provide loans or project finance.

6 References

ADB, 2004. *Vietnam National Workshop on Prega Phase 1*, Workshop Proceedings, Hanoi, December 2004

Beltran, Rick et al. 2005. *Biogas recovery and utilization projects with significant CDM enhancement*, presentation at Workshop on Financing Modalities of the CDM, Jakarta, 27-28 June 2005

CAP SD Energy and Climate Consultants, Pelangi Indonesia, Pusat Tenaga Malaysia, Center for Energy Environment Resources Development, Preferred Energy Incorporated, EcoSecurities Ltd, Hamburg Institute of International Economics, 2005. *Improving the Competitiveness of Southeast Asia on the Global CDM Market.* Regional Cooperation in ASEAN on CDM in the Energy Sector, Discussion paper, Jakarta

Institut Teknologi Bandung, 2002. *Clean Development Mechanism Project Opportunities in Indonesia* - Pre-feasibility Report on a Palm Oil Waste to Energy CDM Project, Bandung

NOCCOP (National Office for Climate Change & Ozone Layer Protection), 2005. *The training workshop on making projects CDM viable technical issues for project develope,r* Workshop Proceedings, Hanoi, April 2005

Matsushita Electric Industrial Co., EX CORPORATION, Kyushu Institute of Technology, 2003. *FELDA Lepar Hilir Palm Oil Mill Biogas Project in Malaysia*, Tokyo

Michaelowa, Axel, 2004. *CDM incentives in industrialized countries - the long and winding road*, International Review for Environmental Strategies, 5, 1, p. 217-231

Michaelowa, Axel, 2003. *CDM host country institution building*, Mitigation and Adaptation Strategies for Global Change, 8, p. 201-220

Nguyen Duc Cuong, 2004. *Biomass for electricity generation in Vietnam, presentation at Information for the Commercialisation of Renewables in ASEAN (ICRA)*, Kuala Lumpur, August, 2004

Nguyen Tien Long, 2004. *Review of renewable energy in Vietnam*, presentation at The Technology Partnership for New & Renewable Energy Meeting, Regional Institute of Environment Technology (RIET), Hochiminh city, March 2004

Plevin, Richard; Donelly, David, 2004. *Converting waste to energy and profit*, Renewable Energy World, Sept-Oct 2004, p. 74-81

State Ministry for Environment of the Republic of Indonesia, 2001. *National Strategy Study on the Clean Development Mechanism*, Jakarta

Vietnam NSS Report, 2004. Hard copy, forthcoming on the World Bank web-site

Small-scale CDM: Potential for Green IPP Development?

Stefan Bakker, Energy research Centre of the Netherlands, Amsterdam

ABSTRACT: The Clean Development Mechanism is currently under rapid development with a fast expanding project pipeline and over 20 baseline methodologies approved by the CDM Executive Board. Over 300 projects have reached the validation stage, of which a significant part small-scale. These small-scale projects may offer an interesting financing option for Green Independent Power Producers to implement renewable electricity projects. This paper briefly outlines the current state of the CDM market in general and for small-scale projects in particular, regarding project pipeline, technologies, host countries. It is shown that transaction cost is a significant barrier towards implementation of small-scale projects under the CDM. Bundling of smaller projects may be an interesting option for reducing transaction cost. Institutional development in host countries has been shown to be a crucial factor in successful CDM project implementation and this is illustrated by two ASEAN countries: Vietnam and The Philippines. The paper concludes with a short discussion of the opportunities for small-scale renewable electricity projects in ASEAN. Biomass and hydropower, particularly in bundled projects, can well be implemented under small-scale CDM, as the technical potential is present. Critical for this is a streamlined project approval process and designation of non-Annex I Operational Entities.

1 Introduction

The Clean Development Mechanism has been designed to help Annex I countries in achieving their target under the Kyoto Protocol more cost-effectively and to promote sustainable development in non-Annex I countries. Till date, it is often considered to have failed to deliver both sustainable development as well as a significant volume of emission reduction. Small-scale projects are decentralised in nature and thus have the potential to contribute more to sustainable development in terms of poverty alleviation and employment generation compared to regular CDM projects but face several barriers to implementation. To fast-track small-scale projects, special modalities and procedures have been designed.

This paper focuses on the opportunities and barriers for green independent power producers to use the small-scale CDM as a vehicle for implementation. Firstly, the current project portfolio will be analysed. The paper goes on to discuss the financial barrier of transaction cost and how this can be reduced. Briefly two case countries, Vietnam and The Philippines will be discussed. The paper concludes by discussing small-scale CDM opportunities for GrIPPs.

2 CDM and Small-scale CDM: Overview

The CDM market is currently developing fast. As of June 2005, more than 100 baseline methodologies have been submitted and the CDM Executive Board has approved over 20. Ten projects have been registered, of which four small-scale. Here we give a brief overview of the current status of the approximately 300 CDM projects of which a Project Design Document (PDD) has been published.

2.1 Technologies

A wide range of technologies is eligible under the CDM. The most relevant difference is the greenhouse gas it aims to abate. It can be seen from figure 1 that methane capture projects (mostly landfill gas) are highest in number as well as greenhouse reduction. A small number of industrial projects abating gases with high global warming potentials, N_2O and HFCs, achieve relatively large GHG reductions. Next are the 'CO_2 projects': energy efficiency, fuel switch and renewables. They all take up a significant share of the reductions and are large in number. GHG reduction for such a CDM project is typically around 1 $MtCO_2$ across 10 or 21 years crediting. It should be noted that the CO_2 projects have in general the largest sustainable development benefits, such as improved air quality, energy security and local employment.

Most projects involving renewable electricity production use hydropower, biomass, geothermal or landfill gas (approximately half of the latter utilise the recovered landfill gas for power generation). Wind energy takes up a smaller share.

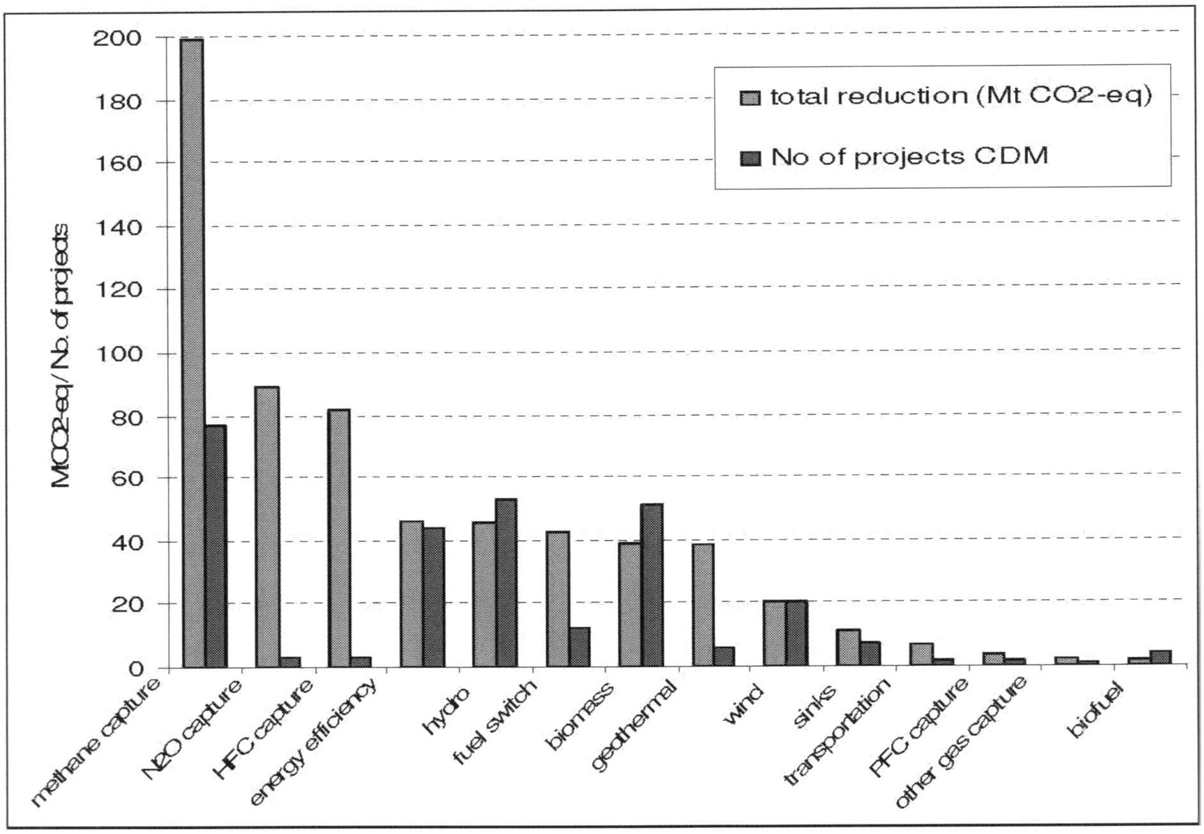

Figure 1: CDM Projects technologie-wise as of July 2005, GHG reductions up to 2025 (ECN Database)

2.2 Host countries

As with technologies, preferences for host countries differ considerably. As shown in figure 2, Brazil and India are the most popular, both in terms of GHG reduction as well as number of project. South Korea has 2 HFC and N_2O projects. After China, taking 8% of GHG reduction, 40 countries follow taking 3% or less each. These countries are mostly in Asia (55%) and Latin America (38%).

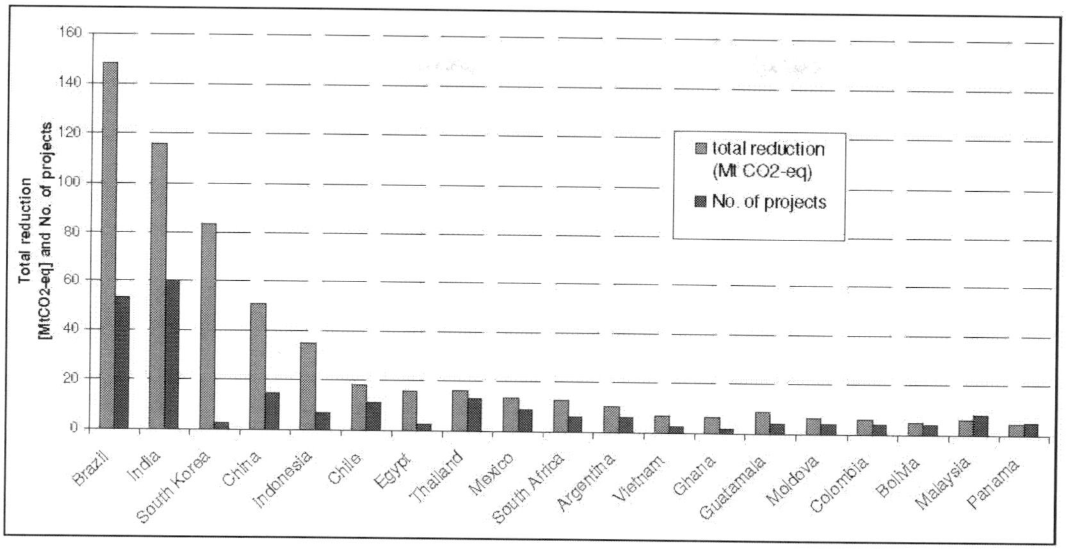

Figure 2: Host country overview of CDM projects as of June 2005 (ECN Database)

2.3 Buyers

Most of the published Project Design Documents mention which Annex I party intends to buy (part of) the Certified Emission Reductions (CERs) the project will generate. In some cases multiple buyers are identified, who share the credits. However since recently so-called 'unilateral' CDM projects, i.e. with no Annex-I involvement up to the validation stage, appear to be on the increase. In this case the project developer will look for possible CER buyers later.

Until recently the Dutch government (CERUPT tenders and other programmes) and the Prototype Carbon Fund dominated the market with over 50 emission reduction purchase contracts (ERPAs). In the past year however, several other funds, countries as well as private buyers have come up. The Japanese government and companies are particularly important with over 20 projects. European buyers include governments and companies from Austria, Finland (especially small-scale projects), Denmark, Sweden, Spain, France, UK and Germany (the latter two mainly private buyers). Canada has also contracted several projects. Finally, a number of credit purchasing funds have been set up: Community Development Carbon Fund (World Bank, small-scale projects), World Bank Carbon Finance Unit, IFC Netherlands Carbon Facility (INCaF), BioCarbon Fund, Multilateral Carbon Credit Fund, Italian Carbon Fund. It should be noted that with the establishment of the EU Emission Trading Scheme, corporate European buyers may also account for a considerable demand of CERs, particularly if carbon prices within the scheme remain at current high levels of over 20 €/tCO_2.

Prices negotiated in Emission Reduction Purchase Agreements (ERPAs) cover a range from 3-8 €/tCO_2, with most projects currently in the middle range (Point Carbon, 2005). This depends technology employed, sustainability criteria, and uncertainty regarding non-delivery of CERs or project risk. Purchasing programmes differ in their preferences and criteria of these factors.

2.4 Small-scale CDM: definition and simplified procedures

The CDM Executive Board has defined three types of small-scale CDM projects, which are summarised in Table 1.

Table1: Definition of Small-scale CDM project activities

Project type	Brief description
Type I	Renewable energy projects with a maximum output capacity of 15 MW
Type II	Energy efficiency improvement that reduce energy consumption, on the supply and/or the demand side, by up to the equivalent of 15 GWh per year.
Type III	Other project activities that reduce anthropogenic emissions by sources, and directly emit less than15 ktonnes CO_2 equivalent annually.

Each project type is further divided into more specific categories, thirteen in total. For each of these, simplified baseline and monitoring methodologies have been developed. Type IA, Electricity generation by the user, and Type ID, Renewable electricity generation for a grid, are the most relevant for Green IPPs.

The simplified modalities and procedures as defined by the CDM Executive Board (UNFCCC, 2002) lower several barriers for projects in the CDM project cycle:

- Project activities may be bundled at various stage in the project cycle, reducing transaction cost (see later);
- Reduced requirements for the PDD;
- Simplified baseline methodologies may be used;
- Simplified monitoring plans and reduce monitoring requirements;
- The same Operational Entity may undertake validation, and verification and certification.

In the light of the current issues regarding baseline methodology development, the possibility of using simplified standardised baselines appears very attractive. For baselines for grid-based electricity other than diesel-generators, the following two options for calculating the grid Carbon Emission Factor (kg CO_2/kWh) exist:

- Average of Operating Margin (average of current generation mix) and Build Margin (average of recent additions); or
- Weighted average emissions (in kgCO_2/kWh) of the current power generation mix.

2.5 Small-scale CDM portfolio

As of July 2005, over 80 small-scale CDM projects have reached the PDD stage (validator has opened the PDD for comments), with a striking share in recent months. In number, this is approximately 25% of the CDM market. In terms of GHG reduction (up to 2012), this share is obviously lower, but still significant: 5% or approximately 30 MtCO_2-eq. This figure should be seen in the context of the many very large regular CDM projects, e.g. the earlier mentioned HFC/PFC/N_2O projects, and most methane abatement projects.

The largest number of small-scale project employs hydropower (31). In terms of GHG reduction, hydro and biomass power each take up approximately 30% of the current small-scale market. Methane capture takes about 1/3 of the market, also shown in figure 3. These projects mainly concern landfill gas recovery and manure management. However, also some biomass-like projects are considered under this type, e.g. saw mill waste for electricity production, where the largest GHG reduction component comes from avoided methane emissions. Five small-scale wind projects have been developed, taking a small 5% share of the market.

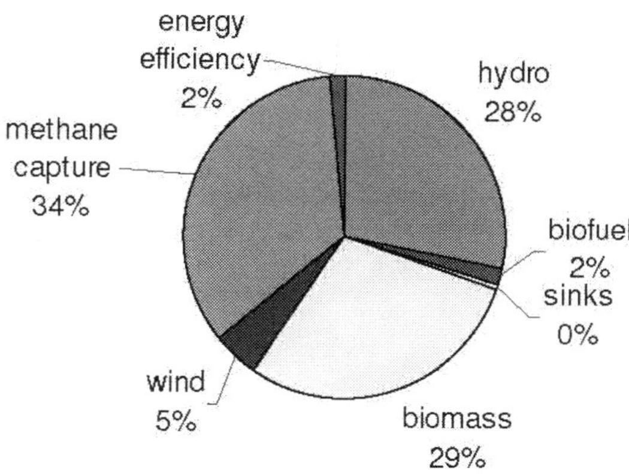

Figure 3: Small-scalec CDM project portfolio as of July 2005, by GHG reduction up to 2012 (ECN Database)

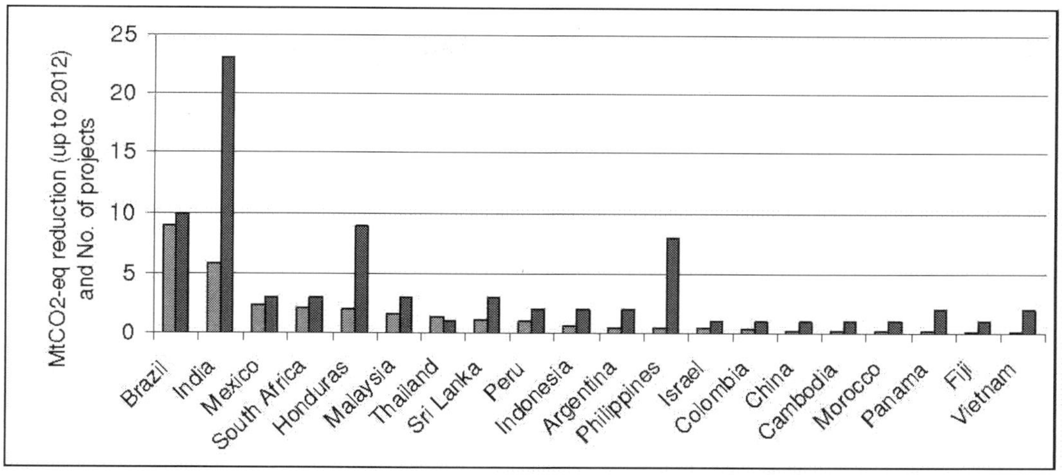

Figure 4: Host country breakdown of Small-scale CDM projects (ECN Database)

Figure 4 shows host countries from the 82 small-scale projects. Compared to Figure 2, significant changes can be noticed. Brazil and India again top the list, but the next seven countries are relatively much more important when it come to small-scale CDM. Particularly striking is the presence of Honduras, where several small hydro projects have been developed for the Finnish small-scale tender. ASEAN countries, the Philippines in particular, are also popular host countries for small-scale projects.

3 Financial Aspects

Finding adequate financial resources is one of the main barriers for implementing small-scale renewable electricity projects. Carbon revenues generated by CDM projects enhances viability, but on the other hand completing the project cycle will use part of this revenue. This section deals with these two financial aspects of small-scale CDM projects.

3.1 Viability impacts due to CERs

Carbon revenues can improve financial viability of small-scale projects in different ways (Gouvello & Coto, 2002):

- Achieve a minimum internal rate of return. CER revenues may be used to improve profitability of the project by covering part of the initial investment cost (by up-front CER purchase agreements) attract private investors by assuring a minimum IRR. Also carbon revenue involves different and reduced risk compared to usual risks in such activities, which helps in attracting investors;
- Help in long-term sustainability of the project. Carbon revenues can be used to cover operating & maintenance cost, which is particularly useful in the case of renewable energy projects;
- Overcoming other barriers, such attract agents more familiar with new technology. This is often a side effect of an international mechanism like CDM.

Viability improvements vary of course considerably across different technologies, which can be seen clearly in the current project portfolio. Low-investment projects - relative to CERs generated - such as landfill gas and N_2O/HFC projects dominate the large-scale CDM market till date. Biomass and hydropower however are also high in number, indicating a significant incentive from the CDM. Wind power on the other hand, with its relatively high initial investment compared to carbon revenues, has a low share. In the small-scale CDM market, we can observe a similar picture, as noted before. For hydro and biomass projects, CER revenues often covers over 10% of power plant investment cost, considering 10 year crediting period, 5 \$/tCO_2 and discount rate higher than 10% (ECN calculations; Gouvello & Coto, 2002). For small-scale landfill gas project obviously this figure is often higher. For wind it is not likely to exceed 10%. Till date no solar power CDM projects have been implemented.

3.2 Transaction cost

Judgement of the validity of the qualification as a CDM project involves substantial effort and cost, which are to a large extent independent of the scale of the project. This is an important barrier for project developers to engage in such project activities (Bhardwaj et al, 2004). However, if the project qualifies for small-scale CDM, significant cost reductions can be achieved by applying the simplified modalities and procedures.

Transaction cost arise from different stages in the CDM project cycle:

- Project appraisal with CDM EB and host country
- PDD preparation
- Validation by OE
- Monitoring

- Verification and certification by OE

The cost of each of these components depends on a number of factors, the most important being monitoring requirements (also depending on project type) and Operational Entity charge. Gouvello & Coto (2002) concluded from an assessment of different studies that for small-scale projects, total transaction cost ranges from 8-80 k$[22] and for normal-scale complex projects 100-1100 k$. Bhardwaj et al (2004) give an estimation for average small-scale transaction cost of 58 k$, which is a 71% cost reduction compared to average normal-scale projects. The up-front cost and the annual cost of monitoring and verification/certification are approximately equal (30 k$ for 10-year crediting period). They have also analysed the transaction cost as percentage of the anticipated CER revenues. For small-scale projects with 10-year crediting time, transaction cost is approximately 5-15%[23] of carbon revenues for projects reducing 30 and 10 kton CO_2-eq annually, at a CO_2 price of 4 $/t. Figures for normal-scale projects (50 - 150 ktCO_2-eq/yr) are in the range of 3-10%. Transaction cost of 10% is generally regarded the maximum for a project developer for submission as a CDM project. It is therefore concluded that for low end (10 ktCO_2/yr) at low CO_2 price, CDM transaction cost is often a too high barrier for small-scale projects. Several options however exist to further reduce transaction cost.

3.3 Reducing transaction cost

Gouvello & Coto carried out a case study for a small-scale hydropower project in Guatemala and concluded that contracting a local OE rather than an Annex-I OE would reduce transaction cost by 70% (78 k$ to 23 k$), and reducing monitoring frequency to once in seven years instead of annually would again decrease the cost by 65% (to 8k$)[24]. Regarding monitoring, Bhardwaj et al (2004) note that in the case of a very large number of small project (i.e. solar home systems), monitoring cost are very high for non-metered projects as compared to metered project, as monitoring guidelines require a sample check on the operational status. Transaction cost for metered project may be 10% of the discounted CER revenues as compared to as much as 69% for non-metered projects (at 30 ktCO_2/yr and 4$/t$CO_2$).

Another important option to minimise up-front and running cost is bundling: combining a number of small-scale project activities into one small-scale CDM project. This can be done in various stage of the project cycle. IT Power & KITE (2002) have shown that by bundling the internal rate of return may improve by 1-3%. Mariyappan et al (2005) have developed a comprehensive guide for bundling small-scale CDM projects. The bundling organisation is the central entity in the bundled CDM project, and needs to make agreements with the project developers, CDM Executive Board, CER buyer and host country, as shown in Figure 5. The bundling organisation as a result runs some extra risks - in addition to those for a 'single' project - related to the number of parties involved and the issue that request for review of one of the sub-projects can impact the entire bundled project. Smallridge (2004) makes several recommendations to minimise risk. This includes using the same technology, technology suppliers, investors, sponsors, operating management, preferably in the same region and falling under the same regional energy plans.

The current CDM project portfolio contains several bundled projects, such as Kuyasa Housing in South Africa (energy efficiency, also CDM Gold Standard[25]), the umbrella project

[22] k$=1000 USD
[23] calculated as total transaction cost divided by total CER revenues across 10 years, undiscounted
[24] Annual monitoring however is required
[25] see www.cdmgoldstandard.org

in Honduras (wind and hydro), 9 biomass gasifiers in India (biomass), umbrella project in Mexico (hydro)[26].

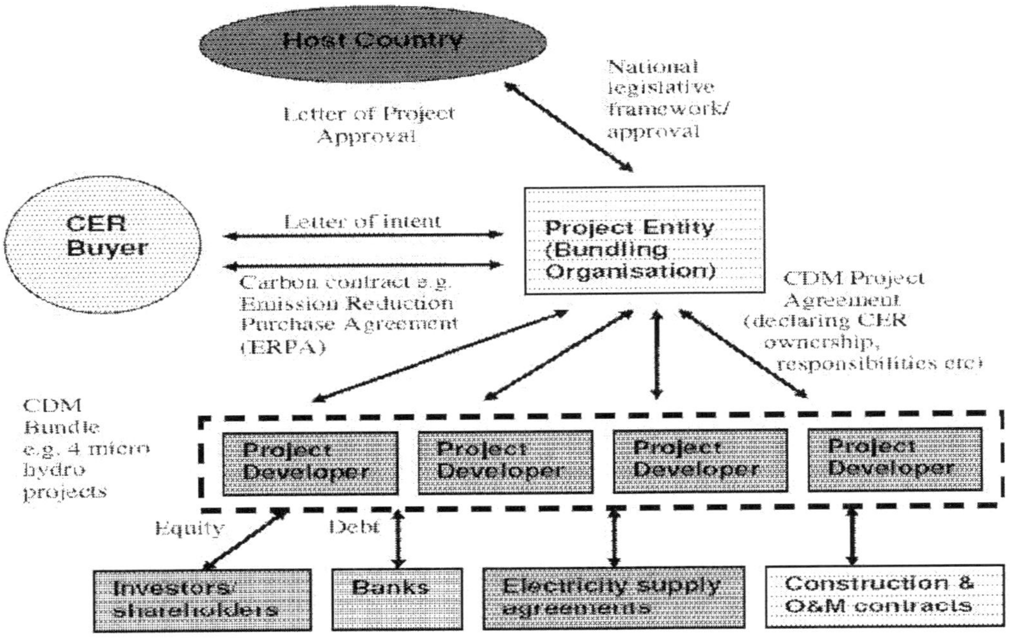

Figure 5: Legal agreements for bundled CDM projects (Mariyappan et al., 2005)

4 CDM development in Vietnam and the Philippines

In addition to financial aspects, institutional development (e.g. in host countries) is required for successful implementation of the CDM project. Institutional barriers are defined as *barriers that are embedded in the institutional structure of the government or of the international agreements that govern the CDM* (Bhardwaj et al, 2004). Over the past few years, a lot of institutional capacity building programmes have operated in non-Annex I countries and developments relating to methodology issue and the CDM Executive Board are going rapidly, while international regulatory CDM framework is almost finalised[27]. This section focuses on two important ASEAN countries regarding institutional development and project pipeline. These are two cases where institutional capacity is quickly developing (but not perfectly in place) and the project pipeline appears to be responding thereto.

4.1 Vietnam

Vietnam ratified the Kyoto Protocol on September 25th, 2002 and the government has formulated a policy towards climate change stipulating its vulnerability and need for developed countries to take the lead in mitigation, but also stresses willingness to participate in CDM. It has assigned the Ministry of Natural Resources and Environment (MONRE) as the National Focal Agency for implementing the Kyoto Protocol. The International Cooperation Department of MONRE is the Vietnamese Designated National Authority (DNA), established in March 2003. The DNA has a range of tasks including formulating sustainability criteria, assessment of CDM projects and overall management and coordination of CDM activities in the country. The minister of MONRE issues letters of endorsement or

[26] see http://cdm.unfccc.int/Projects/Validation/?archive=yes
[27] that is for the first commitment period, not for post-2012

approval to project developers after consultation of a board with representatives from several ministries. The DNA has developed sustainability criteria against which proposed projects are analysed, under which national income generation, technology transfer, air and water pollution reduction, erosion reduction, biodiversity impacts, rural employment, reduction in number of poor people and improvement of living conditions. The CD4CDM project[28] has been active in capacity building and has helped the Vietnamese DNA with several institutional aspects.

Vietnam's CDM project pipeline contains only three projects in the PDD stage (of which one has acquired an approved methodology), all reducing methane emissions. Two of them are small-scale generating 0.2 MtCO2-eq by 2012. However, a larger set of Project Idea Notes (PINs) have been submitted to the DNA. This includes 10 energy efficiency and 11 renewable electricity projects, most of which hydro, but also wind and geothermal. Methane and sinks PINs have also been developed (MONRE, 2005; ECN database).

4.2 Philippines

The Philippines government ratified the Kyoto Protocol on November 20, 2003. Estabilished in 1991, the Inter-Agency Committee on Climate Change has been leading Philippines efforts regarding climate change internationally and locally (Klima, 2005). The CD4CDM has been instrumental in developing the necessary institutions and several sectoral mitigation studies have been carried out, under which the Asian Least-cost GHG Abatement Strategy (ALGAS). The Department of Environment and Natural Resources has been assigned as the DNA. A simplified approval process for small-scale CDM projects has been designed.

In the Philippines 12 small-scale projects have reached the PDD stage, 8 of which small-scale generating 0.5 MtCO2-eq by 2012. Most of them involve methane capture from landfills or livestock with electricity production, and one wind energy project. In the PIN stage are 15 renewable electricity projects - mostly biomass, wind and hydro - but also 8 other including methane projects and sinks (Klima, 2005; ECN database).

5 Conclusions and discussion

The CDM market and institutions are in rapid development. The project portfolio is dominated by non-CO_2 projects involving high global warming potential gases. For small-scale projects, methane reducing projects take the largest share, but renewable electricity projects are also large in number and generation of CERs. Wind power projects are less present.

The most important barriers for small-scale projects specifically are financial: transaction cost compared to CER revenues. The simplified modalities and procedures for small-scale CDM projects provide several options for up-front and operating transaction cost reduction. This increases attractiveness for project developers significantly. In many cases, transaction cost can be kept below 10% of CER revenues, which is an important threshold. For very small projects (<10ktCO_2/a) however transaction cost may be a too high barrier, in particular in the case of non-metered renewable electricity systems. Important options to further reduce transaction cost in the future would be using local Operational Entities and bundling of very small projects into one small-scale CDM project.

---

[28] see cd4cdm.org

From the project portfolio and pipeline, the financial analysis and the two country cases Vietnam and The Philippines it appears that small-scale CDM may provide an important opportunity for green independent power producers. This particularly applies for biomass and hydropower, and to lesser extent for wind, while significant solar development appears unlikely at this moment. However it largely depends on the CDM approval and registration process in general if this potential will be utilised. Another important factor is the possibility to contract local (non-Annex I) Operational Entities. Also reduced monitoring requirements, e.g. multi-annual would reduce transaction cost, bringing down transaction cost to an acceptable level for more projects.

6 Acknowlegdement

I would like to thank Nico van der Linden for his valuable comments.

7 References

Bhardwaj, N., B. Parthan, H.C. de Coninck, C. Roos, N.H. van der Linden, J. Green, and J. Mariyappan, 2004. *Realising the potential of small-scale CDM projects in India.* ECN report ECN-C--04-084, Petten, The Netherlands.

Mariyappan, J., N. Bhardwaj, H. de Coninck, and N. van der Linden, 2005. *A Guide to Bundling Small-scale CDM Projects.* report downloadable from www.cdmpool.com

Gouvello, C. de and O. Coto, 2003. *Transaction costs and carbon finance impact on small-scale CDM projects.* PCFplus Report 14. Washington DC, February 2003.

Klima, 2005. *CD4CDM Philippines.* http://www.klima.ph/cd4cdm/actions/project.htm

IT Power & KITE, 2002. *Bundling small-scale CDM projects.*

MONRE (Ministry of Natural Resources and Environment), 2005. *Viet Nam CDM project pipeline.* Ha Noi March 2005.

Point Carbon, 2005. CDM/JI Monitor 12 July 2005. available from www.pointcarbon.com

Smallridge, D., 2004. *How can bundling of RE projects be done*? Presentation at UNEP ECA conference, Rome, 2004. available at http://www.green-markets.org/Bundling.htm

UNFCCC, 2002. *Simplified modalities and procedures for small-scale clean development mechanism project activities.* Annex II to decision FCCC/CP/2002/Add.3. Downloadable at http://cdm.unfccc.int/Reference/Documents/AnnexII/English/annexII.pdf

Made in United States
Orlando, FL
04 November 2026

90201140R00063